Praise for *Teachi*

Among the greatest unresolved issues within schools is developing great models for implementation: Teaching Sprints *is certainly one of the breakthroughs. This book can make major improvements attainable in schools and classrooms, ironically by focusing on tiny shifts.*

—John Hattie, Laureate Professor
Melbourne Graduate School of Education
Melbourne, Australia

In our work we find that 80 per cent of our best ideas come from leading practitioners. This book is a godsend to this domain of learning from doing. With three big components, and three guidelines to quick action for each idea, Teaching Sprints *helps people to get to action and learn from it quickly. Identify best bets and establish improvement routines. Simon Breakspear and Bronwyn Ryrie Jones have given us a strong framework for action in frantic times.*

—Michael Fullan, Professor Emeritus
University of Toronto
Founder, New Pedagogies for Deep Learning
Ontario, Canada

As someone who works closely with teachers to support their development in a wide range of contexts, I found Teaching Sprints *absolutely inspiring and illuminating. Simon Breakspear and Bronwyn Ryrie Jones have managed to capture the complex process of teacher improvement in an elegantly simple framework with crystal clear underlying principles founded on both practice and research evidence, alongside very practical implementation tools. It's a brilliant concept and I'm sure a lot of teachers and leaders will find this incredibly valuable.*

—Tom Sherrington, Education Consultant and Author
Teacherhead.com
London, UK

Simon Breakspear and Bronwyn Ryrie Jones have such a practical way of combining insights from research and practice to help teachers have the best possible impact in their classrooms. This book is a gold mine of practical, tried-and-tested and evidence-informed strategies for teachers and school leaders who want to improve what they do.

—Danielle Toon, Associate Director
Social Ventures Australia
Melbourne, Australia

Authors Simon Breakspear and Bronwyn Ryrie Jones, informed and supported by fellow practitioners and researchers, deliver a powerful guide for a profession committed to getting better at good work. The Teaching Sprints model is an 'innovation lab in the school'; it is a rigorous, adaptive, and impactful approach to embedding professional learning. Teaching Sprints advocates iterative and sustainable improvement in collaborative professional practice – but it does much more – it demonstrates how to do it!

—Anthony Mackay, President and CEO
National Center on Education and the Economy
Washington, DC

Teaching Sprints *is an important book for anyone who works with teachers on practice improvement. Simon Breakspear and Bronwyn Ryrie Jones provide a simple, flexible process for engaging small groups of teachers in developing their craft of teaching. Using simple, straightforward protocols,* Teaching Sprints *helps teachers to engage with relevant research, to choose one small piece of their craft to change and to make that shift to ultimately improve student learning outcomes. I can't wait to share this book with all teachers in my district!*

—Leanne Peters, Assistant Superintendent
Hanover School Division
Manitoba, Canada

For too long teachers have been asked to change practice outside of the context of the classroom and outside the realm of engagement with students.

Here, Simon Breakspear and Bronwyn Ryrie Jones provide a logical, sensible, and pragmatic approach that enables the busy teacher to improve in the classroom with kids. Start with best bets, practice makes progress, and focus on tiny shifts are the key ingredients to launching doable and long-lasting improvement. This is a brilliant book every teacher, coach, and leader should use as they seek to improve teaching and learning.

—Michael McDowell, Superintendent
Ross School District
Author, *Developing Expert Learners*
Ross, CA

This book delivers exactly what teachers want – a structured, logical and achievable strategy to improve their classroom practice and reflect on evidence of impact.

—Adrian Piccoli, Professor
Director, University of New South Wales Gonski Institute for Education
Former Minister for Education, New South Wales
Australia

Teaching Sprints provides educators with a lens through which to think about and explore their practice in tangible ways. The clearly articulated process facilitates collaborative conversations among teams, with a focus on evidence-informed decisions. The opportunity to practice, adjust and reflect supports teachers' professional learning through ongoing intentional and incremental adjustments over time.

—Barb Isaak, Executive Director
Manitoba Association of School Superintendents
Winnipeg, MB
Canada

As the world turns faster and with increasing uncertainty, we, as educators, need to be agile and excellent. We need to project our professionalism and do everything in our power to ensure that the system we deliver is worthy of our children and their futures. This book is brilliantly researched, incredibly pragmatic and, most importantly, profoundly important in helping us all to meet that challenge.

—**Richard Gerver, Speaker, Educator**
Author, *Education: A Manifesto for Change*
London, UK

As a school principal, I've found Teaching Sprints *to be the most effective way to facilitate teacher improvement. It is simple but powerful because it gives teachers a real sense of satisfaction. Through each Sprint, and sometimes in a short space of time, they see both personal improvement and improvement in their students.*

—**Lindy Smith, Principal**
Trinity Catholic School
Melbourne, Australia

Brilliant! As school leaders we live, eat and breathe school improvement. In Teaching Sprints, *Simon Breakspear and Bronwyn Ryrie Jones give us a practical and effective way to make it happen. I wish they had written this 20 years ago when I was a principal.*

—**Neil Barker, Former Director**
Bastow Institute of Educational Leadership
Department of Education and Training
Melbourne, Australia

Our teachers are proof of the impact Teaching Sprints *has on improving their practice and ensuring impact. Teachers meaningfully engage in* Teaching Sprints *because they know it works.*

—**Kylie Donovan, Principal, and Donna Beath, Deputy Principal**
Hoxton Park Public School
New South Wales
Australia

Teaching Sprints *has enabled our teams of educators to refine and improve their teaching practice by engaging with research. The Sprints process fosters collaborative learning and has been a valuable form of professional development in creating lasting change. I like that teachers reflect on their current practice and then identify areas where they could improve their expertise. The change is evident in the conversations you hear in meetings where the first step is engaging with research to inform the decisions we make. It is not uncommon to hear teachers say, "Well, what is the best way of teaching. . . ?" Sprints has reaffirmed the need for teachers to be continual learners who constantly strive to get better, regardless of their experience.*

—Angela Dobbin, Assistant Principal
Northbridge Public School
Sydney, Australia

As a school leader, I credit the role Teaching Sprints *has had in shaping staff culture – it's one of continual teacher improvement. Through Sprints, teachers at my school routinely improve their effectiveness while simultaneously building strong relational trust.*

—Steven Hooke, Principal
The Oaks Public School
Sydney, Australia

The Teaching Sprints process has become embedded in our school's practice. Teachers collaborate, using the three phases of a Teaching Sprint to research around best practice, implement, review, refine, and assess. Improvement in student learning outcomes is evident as a result of the focus on improving and refining teacher pedagogy.

—Joanne Graham, Principal
Kurnell Public School
New South Wales
Australia

Once in a generation, a process for enhancing teacher expertise is developed that lays an evolutionary foundation for profound growth and improvement. This book offers a breakthrough approach in this area that profoundly focuses on teacher agency, incremental growth every day of the year, and the power of collaborative work in teams. Over the past few years across the province of Alberta, Canada, hundreds of teachers and school leaders have participated in the evolution of the Teaching Sprints process and this has moved teaching expertise forward for both individuals and teams and lifted outcomes for students. I strongly recommend this book for everyone in the profession of teaching.

—Jeff Johnson, Executive Staff Officer
Alberta Teachers' Association
Edmonton, AB, Canada

Teaching Sprints is a great process that allowed our team to have some engaging professional dialogue on our teaching practice. It gave us a safe space to reflect on research and share our learning.

—Kate Foley, Prep One Teacher
Trinity Catholic School
Melbourne, VIC
Australia

Transformative. Timely. Teacher and research informed. Teaching Sprints *provides us with the space for deliberate dialogue around two critical aspects of education: improving student outcomes and shifting pedagogical practice.*

—Karen Graham, Deputy Principal (Instructional Leader)
Blairmount Public School
New South Wales
AUS

Teaching Sprints *has enabled our portfolio of schools/pre-schools to be involved in a consistent organisational process for developing teacher practice and collaboration. As a local education team, the impact of this approach has been clearly identified through the collection of evidence which is enhancing our overall site improvement focus.*

—Adam Box, Education Director,
Partnerships, Schools, and Preschools
Department for Education
Mount Gambier, South Australia
Australia

This book starts with a compelling proposition for anyone involved in teacher learning: "If it doesn't work for teachers, it doesn't work." What Simon Breakspear and Bronwyn Ryrie Jones outline is an evidence-based, field-tested, no-nonsense process to support teachers in continually improving their teaching practice. This is a timely and welcome addition to the teacher learning discourse.

—**Ryan Dunn, Lecturer**
Graduate School of Education
University of Melbourne
Melbourne, Australia

Through Teaching Sprints, thousands of our teachers and leaders now have another, and arguably better, way of moving through a disciplined inquiry process – the intentional experimentation, the fast fails, the iterative improvement. It is these small shifts that have added up over hundreds of our schools to make improvement across a system. We now have more expert teachers who not only know the most impactful teaching strategies, but where and how to use them, for which students, and at precisely the right time.

—**Simon Lindsay, Manager**
Improved Learning Outcomes
Catholic Education Melbourne
Melbourne, Australia

Teaching Sprints are so successful because the core values privilege teacher need and student improvement above anything else. Sprints have transformed our approach to professional learning and teacher growth. We now have a truly authentic and impact driven model for our teachers to engage with.

—**Nicole West, Deputy Principal**
Beaumaris Primary School
Western Australia

Once in a while you come across a book that really cuts through the complexity of issues and provides a refreshing and practical approach *to improving what happens in schools. This is such a book–evidence based, easy to read and full of down-to-earth ideas that busy teachers can implement. I love it.*

—**Steve Munby, Visiting Professor**
University College London
Former CEO, National College for School Leadership
London, UK

It is evident that if we wish to make education systems significantly better, we need to focus simultaneously on transformation of education systems and improvement of teaching. The art of sustainable educational change is to find small steps that will make a big impact in teachers' practice. Teaching Sprints is a book about that. It is a great resource for leaders and teachers who are looking for practical ideas that can improve what teachers do in schools every day.

—**Pasi Sahlberg, Professor of Education Policy**
University of New South Wales Sydney
Author, *FinnishEd Leadership: Four Big,
Inexpensive Ideas to Transform Education*
Sydney, Australia

Teaching Sprints

Teaching Sprints

How Overloaded Educators Can Keep Getting Better

Simon Breakspear

Bronwyn Ryrie Jones

FOR INFORMATION:

Corwin

A SAGE Company

2455 Teller Road

Thousand Oaks, California 91320

(800) 233-9936

www.corwin.com

SAGE Publications Ltd.

1 Oliver's Yard

55 City Road

London EC1Y 1SP

United Kingdom

SAGE Publications India Pvt. Ltd.

B 1/I 1 Mohan Cooperative Industrial Area

Mathura Road, New Delhi 110 044

India

SAGE Publications Asia-Pacific Pte. Ltd.

18 Cross Street #10-10/11/12

China Square Central

Singapore 048423

Acquisitions Editor: Ariel Curry

Associate Content
   Development Editor: Jessica Vidal

Editorial Assistant: Caroline Timmings

Project Editor: Amy Schroller

Copy Editor: Will DeRooy

Typesetter: C&M Digitals (P) Ltd.

Proofreader: Rosemary Campbell

Indexer: Integra

Cover Designer: Scott Van Atta

Library of Congress Cataloging-in-Publication Data

Names: Breakspear, Simon, author. | Jones, Bronwyn Ryrie, author.

Title: Teaching sprints: how overloaded educators can keep getting better/Simon Breakspear, Bronwyn Ryrie Jones.

Description: Thousand Oaks, California: Corwin, [2021] | Includes bibliographical references and index.

Identifiers: LCCN 2020041337 | ISBN 9781506340401 (paperback) | ISBN 9781071840511 (epub) | ISBN 9781071840535 (epub) | ISBN 9781071840528 (pdf)

Subjects: LCSH: Teachers—In-service training. | Teacher effectiveness. | Teachers—Professional relationships. | Teachers—Workload.

Classification: LCC LB1731 .B7234 2021 | DDC 371.102—dc23

LC record available at https://lccn.loc.gov/2020041337

This book is printed on acid-free paper.

MIX
Paper from
responsible sources
FSC® C103567

20 21 22 23 24 10 9 8 7 6 5 4 3 2 1

Contents

More information about *Teaching Sprints* and links to online resources in the book can be found at https://teachingsprints.com.

Preface

Over the last four years, I (Simon) have been working alongside my team, and hundreds of schools, to pioneer a simple and effective approach to teacher professional learning. The research is clear that if we want to improve student outcomes, then helping teachers to get better at what they do is one of the most important responsibilities for leaders, schools and systems/districts. The driving questions from the beginning were simple: *How can we enable overloaded teachers to keep getting better at their craft? How can we build an effective and simple approach to school-based professional learning?*

I had been working with multiple networks of schools across Australia and western Canada in the area of evidence-informed school improvement. Many of these schools were deeply committed to shifting professional learning towards being school-based and practice-focused, but they were struggling to find a way to make it both rigorous and doable for busy practitioners. They had allocated the time for practice improvement and even set up teams and structures, but they were struggling to make it work on the ground.

My team and I have been co-designing, field-testing and implementing a shared process for enhancing expertise within the busy context of school workplaces. We started by examining the critical elements suggested by the best available evidence on effective professional learning (e.g. Cordingley et al., 2015; Timperley et al., 2007; Wei et al., 2009). We identified that the process would need to be job-embedded, support disciplined collaboration, be informed by research, involve intentional experimentation, and generate evidence of impact. We also drew on emerging insights from behavioural science on how to best support adults to make small but important changes to habits and routines (e.g. Duhigg, 2014; Heath & Heath, 2011; Thaler & Sunstein, 2009). In short, the process was designed to enable educators to pursue a sustainable and incremental change approach to practice improvement. Our hypothesis was that if we could help teachers to work on manageable, evidence-informed changes, then these small shifts (what we call Teaching Sprints) could add up to significant improvements in expertise over time. Each small Sprint would only last for about four weeks, but the cumulative effect on teacher expertise, over multiple cycles, could be extremely powerful.

It's been an iterative research, design and development process of trialling, gathering feedback, learning from mistakes and re-testing the model in the field. I got things wrong more times than I would care to admit. I'm very grateful to my school and system partners, who partnered in this co-design and implementation learning journey. From 2017 we also ran three Sprints summits in Sydney to bring together our global community and share our insights into implementing job-embedded, evidence-enriched professional learning models. These gatherings, and the generosity of spirit, were crucial in helping me refine my own thinking.

I am thrilled to now be able to share our collective learning – the Teaching Sprints process – and can't wait to see how you adapt it to improve the quality of professional learning within your unique educational contexts.

I've written this book as a team effort. Since late 2018 I've been working with Bron Ryrie Jones, a brilliant teacher and university teacher educator who has been integral to my effort to refine the Sprints model into something that can work with diverse educators working in a broad range of contexts. We have benefited from the input of an incredible faculty of facilitators and Teaching Sprints practitioners, who have all helped us to pioneer and refine this approach. In this book we have tried to weave together our perspectives and incorporate the rich insights we have gleaned from working shoulder-to-shoulder with frontline educators who have been exploring how to get better at getting better.

We are excited to also welcome you into the Teaching Sprints Community of educators – now 10,000-plus strong and growing all around the globe. We hope that you will find this practical guide a helpful resource as you progress on your practice improvement journey.

Towards better learning,

Simon Breakspear
April 2020

Acknowledgments

FROM SIMON BREAKSPEAR

Books like these emerge due to the collective efforts and generosity of many. I have benefited enormously from the support, suggestions and contributions of educators and leaders from across the globe over the last five years. I've also been grateful for robust conversations and challenge about how to translate the research on evidence-informed teaching, professional learning, expertise and research mobilisation into a practical process that can work in schools.

To my co-author Bron Ryrie Jones, thank you for taking on this crazy project with me to codify the process and synthesise the lessons learned over the years. I am grateful for your deep sense of purpose, sharp eye for detail and relentless commitment to serving teachers by providing ideas and tools that really work for them.

I'm incredibly grateful to those who have been there since the early days when the ideas were still forming. Jeff Johnson from the Alberta Teachers' Association brought together our first networked innovation community to design ideas on school-based teacher learning. Nelson González was the one who originally introduced me to agile ways of working in Silicon Valley and co-delivered early workshops as we adapted a 'sprints approach' to teacher professional learning. Ricky Campbell-Allen was the first core member of our faculty. She helped to build, test and refine our early process and protocols with hundreds of educators.

The refinement of the model was helped immeasurably over the years by a small but mighty team of practitioners and applied researchers. Cale Birk, Terri Lynn Guimond, Corey Haley, Lynne Khong, Ryan Dunn, Bron Ryrie Jones, Kristie O'Neill and Leanne McGettigan have generously provided support, challenge and practical ideas to make Teaching Sprints what it is today. They have reviewed models, tested the process and protocols in different parts of the world, and been the driving energy behind our broader Teaching Sprints Community: thank you! I'm grateful for your friendship, challenge and co-design. You helped the original ideas come to life and become a process that could work across diverse educational settings. Renee Underwood, you keep everything moving in the right direction. Thank you for being the backbone of our team.

I've benefited from deep co-learning partnerships with various systems and networks of schools: various leaders and educators from across Alberta; Simon Lindsay, Shauna-Maree Sykes and Verity Pearson from Catholic Education Melbourne; Barb Isaak and Leanne Peters at the Manitoba Association of School Superintendents; the network of NSW schools that joined the Getting Evidence Moving in Schools (GEMS) Project supported by Danielle Toon at Evidence for Learning; Margot Foster, Deb Merret and Adam Box in South Australia; Ian Anderson and other leaders from the Western Australian Primary Principals' Association (WAPPA); Asmaa Al-Fadala from the Qatar Foundation; Neil Stephenson from Delta School District, British Columbia; John McGettigan, Greg Chatlain, Terri Fradette and Ray Morrison from Saskatoon; and many others who have been on the journey.

Sincere thanks to Alma Ryrie-Jones for your generous feedback and skilled editing as we pushed towards submission of the manuscript.

Most importantly, thank you to my wife Alice for your partnership in all things.

FROM BRONWYN RYRIE JONES

To my co-author Simon and all the wonderful people I've met since joining the Teaching Sprints team two years ago – thank you for welcoming me in. I've learnt so much.

Thanks to my parents Paul and Alma – both teachers – for instilling in me that there is nothing more golden than a good education, and to my Nana Gwen, whose love of learning has stayed with me always. To my parents-in-law, Maria and Lou – thank you for always supporting me.

Thanks to Sharon Marmo and everyone I've taught with over the years at Banyule Primary School; I owe my love of teaching to you. To colleagues in higher education – Associate Professor Narelle Lemon, Nadine Crane, Annabelle Marinelli, Pam Robertson, Emlyn Walter-Cruickshank, Belinda Crowe, Associate Professor Jennifer Clifton and Dr Ryan Dunn – it's because of our friendships (and involved conversations about teaching) that I've co-authored a book on teacher learning.

To my students, past and present – thank you for lighting up my professional life.

To my partner, Brett – in support of this project, you've endured countless consecutive days of COVID-19 lockdown with our toddler; sometimes it's a fine line between support and suffering. I see and appreciate all that you are, and all that you do.

And to our divine daughter, Lucie Scapin Jones – I love you.

CONTRIBUTORS

We are very grateful to the educators listed here, who have generously contributed insights and tips throughout the book.

- Ricky Campbell-Allen, New South Wales, Australia

- Natalie Dolan, New South Wales, Australia

- Terri Lynn Guimond, Alberta, Canada

- Corey Haley, Alberta, Canada

- Annabelle Marinelli, Victoria, Australia

- Leanne McGettigan, Saskatchewan, Canada

- Kristie O'Neill, New South Wales, Australia

- Neil Stephenson, British Columbia, Canada

About the Authors

Dr. Simon Breakspear is a researcher, advisor and speaker on educational leadership, policy and change. He is a research fellow at the Gonski Institute at UNSW in Sydney, Australia. Simon develops frameworks and tools that make evidence-based ideas actionable and easy to understand. Over the last decade, his capacity-building work has given him the opportunity to work with over 100,000 educators across ten countries.

Simon received his BPsych (Hons) from UNSW, his MSc in comparative and international education from the University of Oxford and his PhD in education from the University of Cambridge. He was a Commonwealth Scholar at Oxford and a Gates Scholar at Cambridge. Simon began his work in education as a high school teacher and lives in Sydney with his wife and three young children.

Bronwyn Ryrie Jones is a primary school teacher and a teacher educator at the University of Melbourne (Graduate School of Education). She consults widely across Australia, supporting teachers to develop aspects of explicit instruction and formative assessment. Bron has worked with hundreds of schools and thousands of teachers in metropolitan, regional and rural areas. She regularly consults with the Department of Education and Training (Victoria) and various institutes of educational leadership.

Bron received her Bachelor of Education from RMIT University (Melbourne) and her Master of Education from the Melbourne Graduate School of Education (University of Melbourne). She recently commenced doctoral studies. Bron lives in Melbourne with her husband Brett and daughter Lucie.

▶ Introduction

. . . .

Teaching Sprints is first and foremost about teachers and their learning – the deepening of their pedagogical knowledge, the expansion of their instructional repertoires, and the enhancement of their expertise. While we home right in on teachers and their work, in many ways this is really a little book about improvement.

Whether it's mastering a complex recipe, learning a new phrase in a foreign language, or shaving a split second off a personal best run time, we have all experienced both the grind and the pleasure of improvement. For many of us, achieving new levels of mastery stacks up as one of the most gratifying of all human experiences. While improvement is often rewarding for its own sake, for teachers there is also a clear and moral imperative to improve; we all want to have a greater impact on the students we teach.

For every teacher to have the opportunity to improve, we need approaches to professional learning that work not just in theory, but also in practice. We now know that professional learning has a better chance of being effective if it's school-based, job-embedded, sustained over time and supported by local school leadership (Cole, 2012; Cordingley et al., 2015; Timperley et al., 2007). Stand-alone workshops, conferences and short courses can be useful for building knowledge, but sustainable practice change happens when teachers learn the work by doing the work in the places where they work.

SEARCHING FOR A BETTER MODEL FOR SCHOOL-BASED PROFESSIONAL LEARNING

Over years of working with thousands of teachers and leaders, a few recurring questions began to consume our thinking: How can teachers improve practice in a way that is both robust *and* rewarding over the long term? Rigorous *and* manageable? Meaningful for actual classroom practice *and* informed by the best educational research?

Teaching Sprints is one collective answer to these questions.

We've been developing this approach hand-in-hand with hundreds of schools and thousands of educators. Through the process of developing it, we've been grounded by one simple mantra: *"If it doesn't work for teachers, it doesn't work"*. Because the Teaching Sprints approach has been field-tested and refined with teachers, it's our great hope that it can work *for* teachers. We are always in search of feedback from colleagues in classrooms, and of course we would very much welcome that from you. For the Teaching Sprints process to be better next year than it is this year, we need to know what clicks, what settles well, and what can be refined.

If it doesn't work for teachers, it doesn't work.

We are excited to share this resource with you and we hope it hits the sweet spot for any teacher or school leader – theoretical enough to challenge the way you think about practice improvement, but practical enough to support your work on the ground.

FOR ALL OF US, IT'S ABOUT IMPROVEMENT

In some way, shape or form, all teachers enter the profession ill-equipped for the absolute demands of the job. Indeed, it would seem impossible that any one person could learn all there is to know in any given teacher preparation course. Developing mastery in teaching requires much more than acquiring knowledge – it requires learning from doing.

Once we have been teaching for a while, we all start to "learn the ropes". We build up habits and routine ways of working in the classroom;

we set expectations, launch into lessons, model problems, check for understanding, and provide feedback. At any moment, our current practices are most likely an eclectic amalgamation of tried and tested strategies, techniques that were modelled by our own teachers when we were students, routines we used when surviving our first few years in the classroom, and approaches we developed by imitating trusted colleagues, mentors and experts. While this mix of approaches invariably gets the job done on any given day of the week, it's worth asking ourselves: *What are the odds that this specific collection of practices represents the optimal way to enhance student learning?* In a job as complex as teaching, the odds will always be low.

So it will always be true that *all* teachers can improve. No matter where you are starting from, we think that every teacher can enjoy the full fruits of developing higher levels of mastery – whether that involves replacing a really good strategy with a better one, or fundamentally rethinking the way you have taught something in the past.

THE IMPROVEMENT TRAJECTORY IN TEACHING

In workshops with teachers, we often begin with a simple prompt for discussion: *What is something you do in the classroom now more effectively than you did six months ago?*

As we move around the room, we hear a range of interesting responses.

The early career teacher very easily brings a long list of examples to mind. "I've established much clearer expectations for behaviour, I have strategies to involve the quieter kids in discussions, I am much better at identifying and teaching important background knowledge for comprehension", and so on.

In contrast, the more experienced teacher may struggle to answer the question. They might sit for several minutes, searching their memories for a practice improvement to share. This teacher may well feel that they've been teaching to the absolute best of their ability, but they are often less *conscious* of having improved practice over the last couple of terms.

This observation will make sense to most teachers. We all recall the extreme demands on our learning in the first few years in the classroom;

some of us reflect with horror on all that we didn't know. Naturally, and mercifully, with years of practice we gain confidence, become more effective practitioners, and automate certain practices. Experience is of course *crucial* to getting better, but in a job as complex as teaching, it is not enough. Without the chance to thoughtfully and consciously learn new things, many of us will experience what teacher and researcher Alex Quigley calls a state of "professional inertia" (Quigley, 2013). We gradually flatten the trajectory of our improvement and, without new inputs, can experience what's commonly understood in the literature as a premature plateau of expertise (Rice, 2013; Rivkin et al., 2005). Sometimes described as a level at which we are "good enough", this is the point at which more experience alone is unlikely to have a significant impact on performance (Ericsson, 2006, 2008).

You can think about this in the context of your own cooking.

Think about a "go-to" meal you cook – week in, week out – at home. It might be a spaghetti bolognese, a chicken curry, a vegetable stir-fry, or (for the more challenged amongst us) a humble toasted sandwich. Consider how that dish tasted a year ago. You've cooked it countless times since then, but has the quality of the meal noticeably improved? If you've reached a plateau of expertise, it's likely that more experience, by itself, in cooking the dish has not necessarily enhanced the quality of the outcome. That said, you probably recognise that your spaghetti bolognese – *just* as you cooked it last week – does the job just fine.

This poses a challenge for practice improvement in teaching: we know that experience alone will not necessarily improve outcomes, and we know that the practices we use every day are not all likely to be optimal. But just as we do in the kitchen at home, we already use "good enough" strategies for most (if not all) of the things we do in the classroom. Add to this an enormous workload to juggle, and how many teachers can realistically prioritise improvement work in the normal flow of a working week?

A rethinking of school-embedded professional development must start with an acknowledgment of the human demands of teaching and the critically limited time we have to give to improvement work. Teaching Sprints has been built to help teachers (of all experience levels) get going – and keep going – with small, manageable surges of evidence-informed professional learning, nested in and amongst the pressures of any given school term.

THE REALITY OF THE WORKLOAD

We've never met a teacher with too much time and too few things to do. School terms move at a frenetic pace, and teachers often report feeling overloaded. In this context, it is logical for teachers to focus their energies on getting the job done, rather than working on getting better at *how they do* the job.

There is no judgment here; this just feels like a reality to us. But the danger of living with this pattern – year after year – is that you can settle into "default practices" and flatline in your improvement.

A "SPRINTS" APPROACH

The concept of a "sprint" originated in the technology sector and is used in a broad range of organisations around the world. Thankfully, running a "sprint" in this context involves no physical exercise. Rather we use the term to describe engagement in highly focused improvement work within a tightly framed period of time. While the idea of a "sprint" might be new in the context of teacher professional learning, we think it provides a helpful shared language for describing short, sharp bursts of practice improvement work.

A "sprints" approach to improvement embraces the notion of "massive incremental gains", where seemingly modest improvement goals become the focus for growth. Applied to teacher learning, this way of working supports teachers to work on truly manageable shifts to practice; when sequenced thoughtfully, these little evidence-informed changes can add up to significant improvement over time.

Given limited time for professional learning in schools, this approach also involves a laser-like focus on only those practices that are supported by the best evidence from the field. Over short stretches of intense improvement work (called "sprints"), these evidence-based practices are prioritised.

RUNNING SPRINTS TOGETHER

A wealth of evidence supports the role of disciplined professional collaboration in supporting teacher professional learning (e.g. Campbell et al., 2016; Cordingley et al., 2005; Hargreaves & O'Connor, 2018; Harris et al., 2017). In theory, individual teachers could use a "sprints" approach to pursue improvement goals on their own, but Teaching Sprints is designed to be a collaborative process. Hard thinking and practice-based learning is difficult to do alone; in a social context, teachers can readily share ideas, ask questions, identify challenges to existing practice, draw on the expertise of their peers, and celebrate collective progress. Working together, teachers can also get precise about pedagogical approaches; meaning can be made and shared. So while the notion of a "team" will look different in different schools, we encourage you to embrace the potential of getting better together.

THE TEACHING SPRINTS PROCESS

The Teaching Sprints process is easy to remember and simple to use. It comprises three discrete phases, shown in Figure 0.1.

Figure 0.1 **The Teaching Sprints Process**

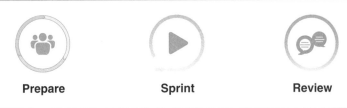

| Prepare | Sprint | Review |

1. **Prepare:** In the Prepare Phase, your team determines which area of practice you want to improve. This involves engaging with the "best bets" from the evidence base and agreeing on intended practice improvements. The Prepare Phase ends when all members of the team commit to practising a specific evidence-based strategy in the Sprint Phase.

2. **Sprint:** The Sprint Phase is all about bridging theory to practice. Over 2 to 4 weeks, team members apply new learning in classrooms through intentional practice. Throughout the Sprint, the team monitors the impact of new approaches, and teachers adapt the strategies based on impact. Supported by a simple protocol, the group meets for a quick, focused Check-in to monitor progress and sustain momentum.

3. **Review:** After 2 to 4 weeks in the Sprint Phase, your team gathers again to close out the Teaching Sprint. During the Review Phase, you reflect on learning as practitioners. The team discusses changes to practice, considers the impact evidence, and decides how new learning will be transferred into future practice.

The three phases of a Teaching Sprint enable teachers to learn about, practise and review a small slice of their teaching over a short period of time. Doing a one-off Teaching Sprint can of course have some benefit, but you will find Teaching Sprints more meaningful if you can embed the process as a regular routine for getting better together.

HOW TO USE THIS BOOK

We hope you use this book like a practical field guide. While we feel confident that what we share has strong support from the research base, we have not set out to write an academic article. So with that in mind, if you want to dig a bit deeper into the literature on teacher learning or evidence-based practices, we encourage you to explore the references. At the time of writing, we have tried to draw on what we think is most useful.

This book will not tell you what you should do in the classroom; nor will it prescribe a rigid procedure for you to follow. Rather, it highlights key concepts in practice improvement and describes an *adaptable process* by which teachers can routinely get better at what they do best.

The book has three parts.

In Part 1, we outline three big ideas of practice improvement for teachers. In Part 2, we provide a detailed overview of each phase of the Teaching Sprints process. In Part 3, we walk you through how to get going with a regular routine for collective improvement in your context.

PART 1
Big Ideas About Getting Better

· ·

n Part 1, we unpack three big ideas about practice improvement in teaching.

1.1   Big Idea 1: Start With the Best Bets

1.2   Big Idea 2: Practice Makes Progress

1.3   Big Idea 3: Focus on Tiny Shifts

Over years of exploring and thinking about teacher learning, we've encountered an ocean of models and a mountain of literature. Putting ourselves back in the shoes of the practising teacher or leader, we've pondered: Which big ideas emerging from the evidence base are most useful for most teachers to know about? What would be immediately helpful for leaders who may be looking for ways to improve the way they do embedded teacher learning?

After a few heated debates and a bit of to-ing and fro-ing, we've settled on three big ideas. While this is clearly not an exhaustive collection of concepts, we hope that together these ideas offer a useful lens through which to review (and improve) job-embedded teacher learning in schools. We certainly hope they are helpful to you.

Figure 1.1   The 3 Big Ideas

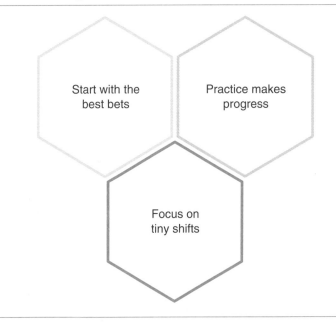

1.1 BIG IDEA 1: START WITH THE BEST BETS

Teachers can only give narrow windows of time to focus on practice improvement; funds and resources for professional learning are critically limited. So how can we make best use of the little time we have? Research evidence plays a central role here.

Because effective teaching is deeply complex (Cohen, 2011), research evidence can never tell teachers exactly what to do at any given moment in the classroom – but it can certainly point us towards the "best bets" (Coe & Kime, 2019; Coe et al., 2020, p. 5). These are the teaching strategies and practices that we know have worked best, on average, in the past and in other places. Teachers need time to learn from experience, but they also need time to learn from those who have formally researched the effectiveness of particular pedagogical approaches (Bell et al., 2010; Cordingley, 2015). Given scant resources and finite time, our view is that teachers should learn about (and become fluent in) only those practices that the evidence suggests have a high likelihood of working with most students, most of the time.

Evidence-Informed Ideas, Not All Ideas

In the positive push to have educators collaborate, there has been a growing tendency to encourage the open sharing of teachers' ideas and practices. While we love the focus on collegial learning, there is an evident danger here. In coming together to talk about what they do, teachers may inadvertently share strategies that are not (or no longer) supported by the most robust evidence from the field. In the absence of research-based inputs, it's entirely possible that we could expend energy working on strategies that are less effective than those we already use, or less effective than the best-known available approaches.

Engaging with quality research evidence helps to avoid this potential pitfall of collaborative teacher learning.

The Emergence of Translational Research

Regrettably, academics in education do not have a good reputation for communicating the findings of their research in digestible or usable formats for teachers. Many researchers do not use relatable terminology; too frequently they do not "speak the language" of teachers. Access also remains a huge issue; important research findings hide behind paywalls. Indeed, much of the most important work of universities – the generation of critical information that could help us progress in solving real-world problems – is not packaged or disseminated in a way that influences teachers' decision-making in practice (Nelson & Walker, 2019; Sharples, 2013).

In light of this, we're fortunate that over the last five years there has been an explosion in both relevant and robust research summaries, translated well for practice, and written with a teacher audience in mind.

In the United Kingdom (UK), for instance, the Sutton Trust and the Education Endowment Foundation (EEF) identify, synthesise and disseminate actionable recommendations in ranging areas of interest for educators. The EEF's guidance reports summarise global findings on various aspects of instruction and school leadership (EEF, 2020), while the Sutton Trust freely publishes research syntheses on everything from teacher testing to local school transport issues (Sutton Trust, 2020). In Australia, Social Ventures Australia has launched Evidence for Learning, a partner of the UK's EEF, which plays an important role in producing localised

Australian summaries and reports. In New Zealand, the Education Hub provides useful teacher-focused summaries of robust research (Education Hub, 2020).

Practising teachers, grassroots groups, allied health professionals and state education systems have also made an impact. Educators can now engage with emerging evidence bases in many ways – at practitioner-led conferences (e.g. ResearchEd, n.d.), via teacher/researcher blogs, and through high-quality and freely downloadable research papers, often commissioned by not-for-profit organisations and departments of education.

The landscape of educational research continues to evolve in the right direction; we think it's easier than ever before to find and make sense of quality evidence.

Evidence Doesn't Replace the Need for Expertise

Research evidence can provide us with good bets for enhancing our impact, but it cannot equip us with the skills to manage the complexity of our own classrooms. The kind of expertise teachers must develop is not simplistic or procedural – it is *adaptive* (Hatano & Inagaki, 1986; Le Fevre & Timperley, 2016).

Experts in teaching are defined as being deeply knowledgeable – not just about what they teach, but how they teach it (Berliner, 1986, 2004; Hattie, 2003; Shulman, 1987). Those with higher levels of adaptive expertise can adjust specific elements of instruction in real time, based on a deep and evidence-informed understanding of both their subject content and how young people learn. They can also think critically about when and why certain teaching strategies tend to work, for whom, and under what conditions. As Professor Rob Coe and colleagues explain, "great teachers need to understand the principles of how and why certain techniques are effective, and when to deploy them" (Coe et al., 2020, p. 15).

So teachers must be given opportunities to learn about effective techniques, but they also need time to consider the principles and theories that underpin them. When teachers understand *why* certain strategies work as they do, they are better placed to judge how and when to use them in context – and perhaps even when to adapt them on the run.

Sometimes in the provision of professional learning, we overlook the importance of underpinning theory; for instance, we might encourage teachers to "use worked examples", without building their understanding of Cognitive Load Theory or the limits of working memory (see Kirschner & Hendrick, 2020, pp. 14–21). Similarly, we might instruct teachers to "use low-stakes quizzes", without exploring important insights from cognitive science that support the use of retrieval practice (for a helpful introduction, see Jones, 2020).

The best bets from the research help teachers to select a focus for their collective improvement efforts – but effective engagement with evidence also requires hard thinking about underlying principles *and* dialogue to tease out what it means for teaching in a unique context. Exploring robust research evidence should also prompt practical action – trying things out in the real world – which leads us to Big Idea 2.

1.2 BIG IDEA 2: PRACTICE MAKES PROGRESS

Engaging with evidence is critical to enhancing expertise, but we mustn't make the common mistake of reducing teacher learning to an intellectual knowledge-building exercise. Acquiring new knowledge is never enough to build expertise; rather, research engagement must kick-start a conscious move into some type of practice. We suspect the role of practising has for too long been overlooked in the organisation and provision of professional learning for teachers, so we view it as indispensable to any model for practice improvement.

We all know and recognise the value of practising. Many of us have lived through the frustration of paying for our kids to go to music lessons, only to find that they won't practise. The music teacher becomes frustrated, your child stagnates in their progress, and you keep paying for the lessons! To progress in any area of human expertise – musical, sporting, culinary, surgical or pedagogical – we must commit not only to acquiring knowledge, but also to intentionally practising for improvement (Colvin, 2019; Deans for Impact, 2016; Ericsson, 2016; Lemov et al., 2018).

Practising as Professional Learning

In workshops with teachers, we often ask them to share a mental image that they associate with the term "professional learning". More often than not, teachers offer up a common vision: they're sitting in a crowded room (usually off-site), listening to someone speak to a long deck of slides. Teachers rarely associate "professional learning" with the act of teaching in their own classrooms. This is hardly surprising, given that the vast majority of formal professional development activity happens outside the classroom and in the absence of students.

We think expecting teachers to improve outside the classroom is a bit like expecting a chef to perfect a new recipe without a kitchen to cook in. A chef may well benefit from reading a recipe, or talking to another chef, but we would expect the real improvement to take place in the kitchen; this is where a chef can trial, adapt and make sense of the techniques required not just to cook a meal well, but to enhance it over time.

Time for teachers to expand their knowledge in the absence of students is of course necessary, but we mustn't lose sight of the fact that what teachers actually do in classrooms plays a huge role in their professional learning.

The Literature on Effective Practice

Swedish psychologist and professor K. Anders Ericsson was renowned for his work in the field of effective practice; he extensively studied the ways in which experts acquire superior levels of performance in various domains (Ericsson & Harwell, 2019). He concluded that "deliberate practice" plays an essential role, determining that it involves:

- moving beyond one's comfort zone,

- working on highly-specific improvement goals,

- engaging in intensive practice activities, and

- receiving (and acting on) high-quality feedback (Deans for Impact, 2016; Ericsson et al., 1993; Ericsson, 2008).

There is broad consensus in the literature that deliberate practice seems to account for a substantial part of the variation in performance between people across a broad range of skill domains (Ericsson et al., 2018), but engaging in deliberate practice isn't clear-cut for teachers. Teachers cannot be guaranteed regular and ongoing access to high-quality expert feedback, and the unpredictable nature of the work also presents a challenge.

What Can Practising Look Like for Educators?

Teachers cannot practise like musicians or athletes; they do not set aside time to train on a practice field, nor can they run drills under the watchful eye of a coach. Though the conditions are obviously different, teachers can still be intentional about parts of their practice in the context of their work. Through *intentional practice*, educators can isolate and develop with precision small aspects of their practice, while teaching at the same time. The important distinction here is that in order to improve, teachers must simultaneously perform their craft *and* intentionally practise a small slice of it.

In order to improve, teachers must simultaneously perform their craft *and* intentionally practise a small slice of it.

Thoughtful provision of time for intentional practice provides teachers with the opportunity to really make sense of theoretical learning. By applying knowledge in practice, teachers can enhance instructional decision-making where it matters most – in the classroom and with the students they teach.

Practising Is Important, but What's Realistically Possible?

We want to elevate the role of practising in teacher learning, but we're also mindful of what's realistic. What kind of intentional practice can teachers prioritise among the competing demands of their working week? We think it's critical to keep practice activities focused and manageable, which brings us to Big Idea 3.

1.3 BIG IDEA 3: FOCUS ON TINY SHIFTS

Almost every teacher we've ever worked with has been very open to improving their classroom practice; many have ambitious goals. But the demands of everyday school life can make it impossible (or make it *seem* impossible) to commit to and sustain big changes. At times, we might ride a wave of motivation that leads to action, but a few days (or weeks) later we can easily slip back into the well-worn grooves of our default practices. So how might teachers make sustainable improvements to their expertise over time?

One Thing at a Time

When we struggle to initiate or sustain a behaviour change, sometimes the best approach is not to try to increase motivation or generate willpower, but rather to shrink the size of the intended change. Applied to teaching, this means embracing a willingness to work on one small and manageable component of your practice at a time. Once you've built proficiency (and fluency), you can always move to the next most important aspect to develop – but it's important that you start small. Of course, developing expertise involves more than gathering isolated teaching techniques, but you can't improve all of your teaching at once; by focusing your energies on specific practices, you can meaningfully develop parts of practice, and then integrate these into your teaching more broadly.

The Cumulative Power of Small Changes

A range of authors (e.g. Clear, 2018; Duhigg, 2014; Fogg, 2020) have recently explored the benefits of making small changes to habits.

In his book *Atomic Habits* (2018), James Clear explores the science of habit formation and change, drawing on the analogy of the cumulative benefits of compound interest in a savings account. Clear explains that dollar amounts deposited from individual paychecks may – in isolation – seem insignificant; but over time, that total compounds to deliver a decent savings sum. Applied to habit formation, Clear proposes, even the most modest of behaviour changes add up significantly over time.

This analogy of "compound interest" resonates with us and we think it's helpful for thinking about improvement work in teaching. One-off engagement with research evidence, or doing one short spurt of practising a new questioning technique might not, in isolation, radically enhance your practice. But if every teacher, in every term of school, systematically develops and sustains one small element of practice, over years the "compounding" effect can be significant (particularly if those small elements are thoughtfully sequenced and are built across teams of teachers).

If every teacher, in every term of school, systematically develops and sustains one small element of practice, over years the "compounding" effect can be significant.

BJ Fogg, the director of the Stanford Behavioural Design Lab, takes a similar perspective in his book *Tiny Habits* (Fogg, 2020). Fogg argues that human behaviour change is usually either a response to a life-changing epiphany (which is rare) *or* a result of incremental changes supported by environmental shifts. Used by a reported 60,000 people, his popular Tiny Habits approach aims to support people to engage in simple, sustainable change by harnessing small steps and environmental triggers.

Examples of "Tiny Shifts" Approaches

You'll find countless examples of this approach in the Fitness section of the App Store. *Couch to 5K*, for instance, is an app designed to take you from "couch potato" to running five kilometres in a couple of months. Programs like this help users to take micro-actions towards an end goal. In the beginning, *Couch to 5K* guides the user through short jogs of just a few hundred metres. Tightly timed periods of jogging are punctuated with walking, and generous warm-up and cool-down periods are included. Off the back of early wins, the user builds and sustains momentum over weeks, always heading out for a run knowing that the app will only ever *incrementally* increase the difficulty of the run. Over just a few weeks, you can enjoy fairly dramatic progress in both your fitness level and your enjoyment of running, while avoiding the false hope of becoming a long-distance runner overnight.

Obviously, the analogy is not an exact fit; lifting the effectiveness of your teaching is far more complex than extending the length of your run. But our intent is to highlight one fundamental truth of human behaviour change: it's tough. Desperately wanting to be a runner isn't enough to make you one. It's the small shifts, the commitment to little bursts of improvement, that get you there.

Once you know the destination (e.g. "I want to improve the way I provide student feedback in mathematics"), it's helpful to recognise that it is not *ambition* that will get you there, but the thoughtful mapping of small evidence-informed improvements, worked on over time, in a way that is sustainable and perhaps even pleasurable. It's important to remember that motivation often emerges *as an outcome* of making progress, not the other way around. It is commonly not the end goal, but rather those rewarding visible steps we take along the way, that spur us on in our efforts.

Establishing challenging goals for your professional improvement is important, but go after modest changes; choose them wisely, put them in the right sequence, and rely on the rewards of progress to take you forward.

SUMMARY OF PART I
Big Ideas About Getting Better

Big Idea 1: *Start With the Best Bets*

We have critically limited time and cognitive bandwidth for teacher learning, so we shouldn't waste it on ideas that probably aren't powerful enough to improve student learning. The research base can point us to the best bets for improving practice.

Big Idea 2: *Practice Makes Progress*

To bridge learning to practice, teachers must have the opportunity to apply new learning through intentional practice. To enhance their expertise, teachers must move beyond acquiring new knowledge and into periods of trialling, adapting and refining in the classroom.

Big Idea 3: *Focus on Tiny Shifts*

Working on small shifts to practice allows you to manage the human limits of improvement work. Planned and enacted in the right sequence, incremental changes can add up to appreciable improvements over time.

FURTHER READING

In Part 1, we've explored three core ideas about getting better. If you'd like to do further reading, we recommend these open-source articles about teacher learning and teacher expertise:

Practice With Purpose: The Emerging Science of Teacher Expertise (Deans for Impact, 2016)

Expert Teaching: What Is It, and How Might We Develop It? (Mccrea, 2018)

Teacher Professional Learning and Development (Timperley, 2008)

How Does Professional Development Improve Teaching? (Kennedy, 2016)

You can download these readings at www.teachingsprints.com/teacher learning

Reflection Activity
3 Big Ideas About Getting Better

Reflecting on Big Idea 1: *Start With the Best Bets*

On what research evidence do you currently base your professional learning? How might your team (or school) better engage with robust research evidence as part of your practice improvement work?

_____

_____

_____

_____

_____

_____

Reflecting on Big Idea 2: *Practice Makes Progress*

To build expertise, we need opportunities to apply our learning in classrooms, but this step is often missed in traditional professional learning activities. How might we move from learning about effective practices to intentionally practising them in classrooms?

_____

_____

_____

_____

_____

_____

Reflecting on Big Idea 3: *Focus on Tiny Shifts*

Identify one professional learning goal you have. How might taking a "tiny changes" approach support you to work on improving this area of your teaching?

_____

_____

_____

_____

_____

_____

PART 2
The Teaching Sprints Process

· ·

Over years of working in diverse schools and settings, we've encountered countless models for embedded teacher learning. Colleagues have told us that many models are not all that easy to use; one said they felt perpetually lost in a nine-step cycle of inquiry. Others have told us they're frustrated by poor usability for teachers; one middle leader said she found one process to be so convoluted that it was impossible to explain to her team. Another trusted colleague once confessed that she was "supposed to use a process for collaborative learning", but that senior leaders were the only people in the school who seemed to know much about it.

There is good reason for schools to use processes; without common ways of working, it's hard to do meaningful improvement work together. But we think that any model for a teacher's professional improvement should be simple enough for teachers to follow, interpret and use. We advocate not for something *simplistic*, but rather for something more elegant and friendly to the user.

In Part 2, we introduce you to the adaptable Teaching Sprints process. We hope it gives you and your team a simple and coherent way of working towards the ongoing goal of developing your thinking and teaching, in every term of every school year.

The Three Phases of the Process

A Teaching Sprint has three distinct phases: Prepare, Sprint and Review (see Figure 2.1).

We use the word "phase" to describe a period of time in which teachers are engaged in particular kinds of thinking and working. While the overarching goal of every Teaching Sprint is to develop expertise, each phase involves a different mode of learning.

Phase	Mode of Learning
Prepare	Evidence-informed knowledge-building and disciplined dialogue
Sprint	Intentional practice in classrooms
Review	Collegial reflection and determining implications for future practice

Improvement work of course does not end once teams have moved through a single Teaching Sprint. Continuous professional growth can occur only when teams engage with the process over and over again. While this is flexible, we find that in most settings teachers can comfortably complete one productive Teaching Sprint in every term of school.

Each phase of a Teaching Sprint is supported by a Sprint Leader. In Part 3, we explore in detail the associated roles, possible team compositions, and scheduling suggestions for each phase.

The Bedrock of Big Ideas

Before we head into the specifics of the process, we want to say that in many ways we are happiest when Teaching Sprints is conceptualised as one possible synthesis of some good ideas about practice improvement. We've field-tested this approach with more than 10,000 educators, and we think it's neater, more workable and more elegant than many other models for teacher learning. But we also know that schools are complex ecosystems, and implementation of processes can be variable.

In Part 2, we want to detail the Teaching Sprints approach while warning against fixating on minutiae within the process itself. This seems counterintuitive, but as we switch focus from a conceptual exploration to the specifics of an approach, it may be easy to get bogged down in

Figure 2.1   The Teaching Sprints Process Overview (see also Appendix A)

Prepare

Come together to determine a focus for practice improvement

In this phase, teachers:

- Engage in new learning, informed by research evidence
- Draw out connections and challenges to practice
- Determine a precise strategy/technique for practice improvement

Sprint

Intentionally practise in classrooms

Over 2 to 4 weeks, teachers:

- Intentionally practise the chosen strategy/technique in classrooms
- Make adjustments, in light of what's happening
- Check in with colleagues to sustain momentum

Review

Reflect on the process and learn from each other

In this phase, teachers:

- Reflect on the effectiveness of the Sprint
- Share insights and determine implications for future practice
- Identify possible next steps for professional learning

relatively unimportant mechanics. Of course, a clear model for teacher learning can be helpful in busy schools, but remember that Teaching Sprints is one bringing-together of good ideas, not a sequence of steps to be rigidly followed.

With this in mind, before you head into Part 2, we encourage you to spend some time deeply exploring the ideas outlined in Part 1. We think that if you're equipped with solid knowledge of the big ideas, you'll be much better placed to use, adapt or sidestep elements of the process in a way that will work best in context.

Remember that what is most important is not that you "do Teaching Sprints", but that you develop your own thinking about how to do practice improvement *better* – in your classroom, across your school, or throughout your system.

The Teaching Sprints Process

2.1 THE PREPARE PHASE

In the Prepare Phase, over one or two meetings, teachers turn off autopilot and come together to explore opportunities for improving practice. In this phase, there is a central question to answer: In a sustainable and doable way, what is one technique or strategy we can trial that is *likely* to pay off for our students?

After identifying a broad area of practice area for improvement (e.g. formative assessment or questioning), teams engage with relevant research that has been translated for a practitioner audience. They discuss the evidence in light of their current practices and theories about learning. The goal is to build a richer understanding of the evidence base, select a specific strategy or technique, and commit to trialling it in classrooms.

During the Prepare Phase, teams work through a short sequence of steps:

1. Engage in new learning, informed by research evidence.

2. Draw out connections and challenges to practice.

3. Determine a precise strategy/technique for practice improvement.

Tip From Our Team

The Prepare Phase is about real professional dialogue – the nuts and bolts of teaching, grappling with evidence and then determining a small teaching strategy or technique we will all try in our classrooms.

– Ricky Campbell-Allen (senior faculty, Teaching Sprints)

Step 1: Engage in new learning, informed by research evidence

The Prepare Phase kicks off with teachers exploring evidence and building knowledge together; importantly, this mode of learning sits at the *front end* of Teaching Sprints, and it commonly might involve teachers doing the following:

- Reading a short article together

- Closely examining one evidence-informed principle of instruction

- Listening to an educational research podcast

- Reading an excerpt (or chapter) of a research-based book

- Watching a recorded lecture or teaching demonstration together

- Reading a teacher/researcher's blog which summarises or explores robust evidence findings

Locating high-quality research isn't always easy, so we've developed the Teaching Sprints Research Hub; it's by no means an exhaustive collection, but we hope it helps if you're looking for somewhere to start.

Teaching Sprints Research Hub: At https://teachingsprints. com/research, you can find a curated list of quality open-source materials that are useful inputs for the Prepare Phase.

Making Sense of Research Evidence

As you and your team engage with the research, you might pause to make sense of the material, asking some of the following questions:

- What are the most important messages/concepts emerging?

- What have we found out that we didn't know before?

- What do you think about that, and what do you find interesting?

To run a Research Jigsaw with your team, download the protocol at https://teachingsprints.com/protocols.

Breaking It Down With the Research Jigsaw Protocol

If you choose a meaty piece of research to read (e.g. a whole book chapter or several practice principles), you might want to "chunk" the work by using a simple Research Jigsaw Protocol (see Appendix B). This protocol supports individual teachers to explore smaller excerpts of research; as a team, you are then able to share findings and make sense of new learning together.

Step 2: Draw out connections and challenges to practice

Flicking through a research paper or sitting through a PowerPoint presentation is rarely sufficient to change practice (Sharples, 2013, 2017). Instead, teachers need time to grapple with research as *practitioners* before moving into phases of intentional practice (in situ).

Because of constraints on time and the tacit nature of teacher expertise, we don't often have a chance to make explicit some of our implicit assumptions about practice. *Why do we normally do what we do? Why do we think it works best? How are our approaches challenged or supported by the finest research evidence from the field?* The Prepare Phase provides a structure for teachers to engage with some of these important questions.

Drawing Out Connections to Practice

Once your team has established meaning from the research evidence, it's important to start identifying links to regular classroom practices. Together, you might consider these questions:

- To what extent does this align with what we already do?

- Do we have a shared view of what we do in this area of our teaching and why?

- If we wanted to improve in this area of our teaching based on what we've learned, what could we try first?

Identifying Challenges to Existing Approaches

Teachers do not engage with professional learning as blank slates; they cannot simply "add" instructional practices to enhance their expertise. In fact, most of the time the reality of adopting a new way of working involves replacing an existing pedagogical approach. In the Prepare Phase, it's helpful to identify these challenges to practice.

Together, you and your team might consider several questions:

- To what extent does this evidence challenge the way we usually work?

- Given the evidence, what strategies do we currently use that may actually *not* be optimal?

- Given the evidence, which strategies might we need to sideline (or retire altogether)?

Reconsidering Practices With the Learn & Let Go Protocol

In light of the research evidence, use the Learn & Let Go Protocol (see Appendix C) to collectively determine the approaches that may need to be adjusted, sidelined or stopped.

To run Learn & Let Go with your team, download the protocol free at https://teachingsprints.com/protocols.

Practitioner Insight

The Teaching Sprints protocols have added precision and richness to our Prepare meetings by helping teachers to plan clear and specific Sprints. We've found that the use of a protocol removes individual ego, inviting a less personal but more disciplined kind of conversation.

– *Terri Lynn Guimond (principal in Alberta, Canada)*

Step 3: Determine a precise strategy/ technique for practice improvement

In the last step of the Prepare Phase, teachers determine a specific technique or strategy they will trial in the Sprint. Rather than continuing a long and drawn-out discussion about the research evidence, here teachers spend a few minutes making a decision about what they will intentionally work on in classrooms. It's helpful to get specific now; where possible, you want to narrow the options and determine very precisely one agreed technique to try.

You May Need to Limit the Scope of the Commitment

It's easy to commit to large-scale, earth-shattering efforts – until you need to follow through. Lofty aspirations do not necessarily put us on the path to sustainable change, so it's important to keep reducing the scope of the commitment until it feels manageable for everyone to develop – in and around the regular demands of any given working week.

If the commitment you are making seems too modest for a Sprint, it is probably about the right size. Committing to incremental practice change allows you to meaningfully sequence small shifts which can add up to appreciable gains over time.

Narrowing the Focus With the Boulder, Pebble, Sand Protocol

To run Boulder, Pebble, Sand with your team, download the protocol at https://teachingsprints.com/protocols.

To help your team get to the right "grain size" for a Sprint, you might like to use a simple protocol called Boulder, Pebble, Sand (see Appendix D). *Boulder* is used to describe a broad aim, *Pebble* describes a principle or strategy, and *Sand* a tiny shift that everyone can practise with precision in their classrooms.

Practitioner Insight

The Boulder, Pebble, Sand Protocol is regularly used in our schools. We have found it to be very helpful in determining the right grain-size for changes in practice, leading to more impactful collaborative efforts by our teachers. In my work, I've often struggled to help teacher teams identify manageable levels of change, as well-intentioned teachers try to change too many things at once. Now we regularly talk about 'sand-level' changes, which often reduces some of the pressure teachers feel when considering how to improve teaching practice.

– Neil Stephenson (director of learning
services in British Columbia, Canada)

Establishing With Clarity the Technique to Be Practised

Once you've agreed on a specific technique to trial in the Sprint, it's time to get clear on what it will look like in classrooms. Too often, we speak generally about what we would like to get better at (e.g. questioning), but we never get a good feel for what it would look or sound like if it was done with fidelity. Once you and your team have chosen a technique, we recommend you spend a few minutes determining what the practice will actually look like. What will the teacher say? What will students be doing? What are we *not* going to do in place of what we will trial?

Getting Precise With the Picture of Practice Protocol

To support this kind of conversation, you might like to use the Picture of Practice Protocol (see Appendix E).

To run the Picture of Practice with your team, download the protocol free at https://teachingsprints .com/protocols.

Selecting the Right Protocol for the Right Conversation

It's common for teams to move through the Prepare Phase without using any protocols. We developed them because we think protocols bring discipline to particular kinds of conversations, but it's entirely up to you whether you use them. You can use the Research Jigsaw Protocol to chunk and make sense of larger pieces of research; you can use the Learn & Let Go Protocol if you want to identify existing practices that are less optimal; you can use the Boulder, Pebble, Sand Protocol if you need help getting to a small and manageable technique to trial; and you can use the Picture of Practice Protocol if you think your team needs clarity around an instructional approach. In our experience, teachers who understand the specific purposes of the protocols can better judge when (and when not) to use them.

Summary of the Prepare Phase

In the Prepare Phase, teachers come together to move through three steps:

1. Engage in new learning, informed by research evidence.
2. Draw out connections and challenges to practice.
3. Determine a precise strategy/technique for practice improvement.

2.2 THE SPRINT PHASE

Now the mode of learning shifts to *doing*. The Sprint Phase is the dedicated time in which teachers make a conscious effort to practise the agreed strategy or technique. Here, you and your team are trying to bridge "knowing better" and "doing better"; the beauty of the learning here is that it's truly job-embedded.

During the Sprint Phase, over 2 to 4 weeks, teachers work through a short sequence of steps:

1. Intentionally practise the chosen strategy/technique in classrooms.
2. Make adjustments, in light of what's happening.
3. Check in with colleagues to sustain momentum.

Step 1: Intentionally practise the chosen strategy/technique in classrooms

During the Sprint Phase, within a period of 2 to 4 weeks, you'll need to carve out small, tightly framed chunks of time in which to practise new strategies. Within the allotted time for intentional practice, your teaching should feel more deliberate and effortful than regular, everyday teaching. By the very nature of learning something new, you shouldn't feel like you're on autopilot – rather, you should feel that what you're doing is (in some way) "against the grain" because it is challenging your default practices.

The difference of course is not that you're necessarily doing more or something additional, but that you're doing things *differently*. To build new habits in the classroom, we have to first spend time bringing conscious intentionality to the work. This can feel uncomfortable, particularly if you have to unlearn a deeply ingrained habit to make way for something better.

Each team (or teacher) will need to determine the duration and regularity of intentional practice, depending on what you're seeking to improve. What's key is that you don't attempt to practise every part of your teaching for a month! The Sprint should involve practising just a small slice of your teaching, so as to keep the practice intensive *and* manageable.

Harnessing Expert Resources

Ideally, all teachers would have access to classroom observations, demonstrations and feedback from an expert. These resources are not often available, but in some cases, you may have access to experts (leaders, colleagues or external advisors/consultants) – the Sprint Phase is certainly a good time to tap into these sources of expertise. Although peer observation can be helpful for reflecting on practice, domain-specific experts are best placed to provide feedback and guidance on implementation in the Sprint Phase.

Scheduling Peer Observations

Depending on the focus of your Sprint, having a peer observe in your classroom can be useful for the purpose of collecting evidence of impact. If you invite a colleague in to observe and provide insights, it's important that you (the teacher who will be observed) clarify with the observer exactly what you'd like to know. If you're trying to extend the wait time you give after every question, this might be a matter of your peer counting the seconds that elapse between your asking a question and your seeking a response. In this way, the process of peer observation can be helpful for gathering evidence about the possible impact of your changed teaching.

Step 2: Make adjustments in light of what's happening

The Sprint Phase is about stretching yourself slightly beyond your current level of competence, so you shouldn't expect everything to "click" right away. In light of student responses or expert feedback, you may need to tweak, rethink or adapt strategies on the run. This is a context-specific and complex part of the process; it will invariably look different in different classrooms. It may involve making real-time adjustments or taking time to reflect on what is working and what refinements could be made. You may even consider taking short, sharp video or audio recordings of relevant segments of your teaching to support your personal review of the extent to which you are making the intended changes.

Collecting Evidence of Impact

Although the research base can point us in the direction of instructional best bets, we cannot know whether a practice has been effective if we do not pay attention to outcomes in the classroom. So it's important to gather some evidence of impact as you move through the Sprint. This might include (but is not limited to) observations, checklists, conversations with students, short diagnostic assessments, photographs of student work, full work samples and responses to quizzes.

In some ways, potential sources of impact evidence are endless, but what's most important is that you and your team make a *reasoned* decision here. When thinking about what impact evidence to collect, we think it's helpful to draw on the concept of "decision-driven data collection" (Wiliam, 2014). Wiliam argues that teachers should focus not on the *forms of data* to collect, but rather on the *decisions* that need to be made (or the conclusions that need to be drawn). By attending closely to the decisions to be made, Wiliam argues teachers will be more likely to collect the right amount of the right information. So consider carefully what you want to know, and then collect only evidence that is likely to have a bearing on the conclusions you're hoping to draw.

It's easy for evidence collection to become burdensome for teachers. In Teaching Sprints, you and your team are making incremental shifts to practice, so keep it lean and collect only what you need.

Step 3: Check in with colleagues to sustain momentum

Anyone who has been in a book club can attest to madly trying to finish a book ahead of an upcoming gathering, due solely to the motivational influence of an impending meeting with friends. In a similar way, the Check-in meeting provides a powerful nudge to help you follow through on the specific techniques you committed to trialling; it's also a chance to review what's happening and get supports if you need them. The life of a teacher is busy; if you left it a whole term, your practice improvement commitments could very easily slip to the bottom of the priority list. Running a Check-in meeting provides a source of positive pressure and support which is helpful for everyone.

Tip From Our Team

I often say the Check-in is the "special sauce" of Teaching Sprints for two reasons. Firstly, it helps to motivate team members, as we are held accountable to each other. Secondly, it provides an awesome opportunity to learn from another teacher and tweak teaching practices while you're still working on them, rather than at the end.

– Ricky Campbell-Allen (senior faculty, Teaching Sprints)

Scheduling a Check-in

Schedule at least one Check-in meeting (face-to-face or online) at a helpful point in the Sprint Phase. We recommend scheduling this ahead of time, so that everyone in the team knows when they will meet. A Check-in should last no longer than 15 minutes; it's an opportunity to touch base, not a long or drawn-out meeting. Check-ins should be strictly timed and supported by the Check-in Protocol (see Appendix F).

Questions in the Check-in Protocol (see also Appendix F)

Done

- How are we progressing with the new strategy/technique?

Stuck

- Is anybody stuck?
- Does anyone need resources or support?

Tweak

- What adjustments can we make in order to increase the effectiveness of the Sprint?

If you run this protocol in person, we suggest you facilitate it with a countdown timer visible and with everyone standing up. The idea is to move through the Check-in Protocol questions as quickly as possible and to stay firm on the time limit. No matter what you've discussed, at the end of 15 minutes, the meeting ends. If complex problems emerge, we recommend the Sprint Leader takes note of them but puts them aside for a follow-up discussion.

If you have time, round out the Check-in meeting with a quick "shout-out". Whether it's sharing of practice, responsiveness to feedback, or openness to trialling new techniques, take a short moment to acknowledge the great work that's being done across your team.

Practitioner Insight

If you are like most of the teachers and administrators that I have worked with in schools, work is pretty darn busy. It is easy to get caught up in the cascade of demands put on you by students, parents, administration. . . . Oftentimes, the goals that we have set for ourselves quickly vanish in the daily grind. What if there was a way to focus more on the important things that you want to accomplish? The Check-in helps you do exactly this.

The beauty of the Check-in is that it's simple. It keeps you continually focused on your most important goals, but [it] also lets your Sprint Leader remove any blockers or impediments as you go. The work you're doing in Teaching Sprints makes you a better teacher and your school a better place for learning. This is worth making a small amount of time for.

– Corey Haley (principal in Alberta, Canada)

Summary of the Sprint Phase

During the Sprint Phase, over 2 to 4 weeks, teachers work through a short sequence of steps:

1. Intentionally practise the chosen strategy/technique in classrooms.

2. Make adjustments, in light of what's happening.

3. Check in with colleagues to sustain momentum.

2.3 THE REVIEW PHASE

After 2 to 4 weeks in the Sprint Phase, teachers come back together to review what happened. In the Review Phase, your team takes the opportunity to meet and to make sense of your practical experiences in the classroom. The mode of learning here shifts from action, back to collegial discussion, this time with a focus on drawing out implications for future practice and generating new insights.

Teams can use these guiding questions to reflect on their efforts:

1. What was our experience of the Sprint?

2. What can we reasonably conclude from the impact evidence we have?

3. What are the implications for practice?

4. What are the next steps for our professional learning?

These guiding questions are explored in some depth below, but to facilitate the Review meeting itself, we recommend using the Review Protocol (see Appendix G).

Question 1: What was our experience of the Sprint?

It's one thing to commit to develop your teaching, but often it's a very different thing to enhance practice with students in the room. As you kick off with Question 1, be open to the fact that your colleagues will have had varied experiences: some may have been very intentional in their practice; others might describe the practice change as "awkward", "really hard" or "ineffective". Here, what's most important is that team members have the chance to share their experiences in a non-judgmental environment.

Question 2: What can we reasonably conclude from the impact evidence we have?

To move beyond immediate feelings about the Sprint, it's useful to examine the sources of impact evidence you have; these may be observational notes, descriptions of observed student responses and behaviours, photo or video capture of student work, or perhaps some relevant notes taken by an expert observer. Before anyone makes any strong claims about impact, it's important to acknowledge that, in the classroom, it's nearly impossible to prove that any one small practice change has *caused* any one outcome. Still, it's important to think about what you set out to do, and what you can reasonably infer from the evidence you have.

As part of your evaluation, you might consider whether particular students (or groups of students) seemed to particularly benefit from the change to practice; exploring possible reasons for this can be an interesting part of the review.

Question 3: What are the implications for practice?

One goal of a Teaching Sprint is to intensively build confidence and proficiency with an evidence-informed practice; but the longer-term aim of Teaching Sprints is to apply these improved practices, where appropriate, more broadly in your teaching. In this part of the Review meeting, we turn our attention to the implications for our teaching as a whole: What have we learnt about our practice? Could this strategy or technique be applied in multiple ways? What does it tell us about how students learn best? What do we know now – about students – that we didn't know before?

At this time, teachers should be encouraged to share new ideas about why, when and how strategies/techniques may work best in the context of their classrooms.

Question 4: What are the next steps for our professional learning?

Forming new instructional habits is hard, and all professional learning takes time. At this point in the Review meeting, teachers talk about what they might need next to further their professional learning.

Depending on the outcomes of the Sprint, teachers may like to further their development in one or more ways:

- Continue intentionally practising the technique (to build fluency)

- Attend a demonstration lesson so that they can see the technique in flight (particularly helpful if there is a lack of clarity about what it looks like when it works well)

- Invite an expert observer in to provide further feedback

Teachers within the group may well want to continue work embedding new instructional habits – and, of course, part of this may involve supporting their colleagues to do the same – but it's important to bring each Teaching Sprint to a close. It can be dispiriting if the Review Phase drags on, so try to end on a positive note by keeping it tight.

Practitioner Insight

Don't underestimate the power of celebrating success. As teams, it's important to pause and identify the progress we've made through intentional practice efforts.

– Kristie O'Neill (professional learning coordinator in New South Wales, Australia)

Closing Out the Teaching Sprint

The Review meeting should help you close out one Sprint Phase; it is not designed to support the planning of the next Teaching Sprint. The urge to move on or switch the focus can be a huge point of frustration if teachers are only just getting the hang of a new way of working. We recommend that you allow sufficient time for teachers to consolidate practices before turning your attention to the next Teaching Sprint. By all means, capture ideas – but try to avoid rolling from one Sprint into the next.

Maintaining a Focus on Your Learning

The core goal of any single Teaching Sprint is the enhancement of teachers' expertise, but in reality it can be easy to lose sight of that. We remember chatting to a group of teachers who told us that their first Teaching Sprint had "failed". When pressed to explain why, the teachers said they had worked hard to make an evidence-informed change to practice but that only a small sub-group of students had progressed in their learning. The teachers said they'd been thinking hard about it since, but hadn't yet reached consensus about why the Sprint had been ineffective. When asked why they considered it to be a failure, one teacher said, "because it didn't go as well as we'd hoped".

If teachers have thought more deeply about a slice of their teaching, or engaged with good research that's challenged their existing ways of working, or developed a more nuanced understanding of their impact, then the Sprint has not "failed". The goal of a Teaching Sprint is not to secure perfect practice or to improve student outcomes overnight; it is to stimulate the kind of thinking and action that can generate expertise over the long term. When given *this* definition of purpose, the teachers realised that their practice improvement work had not been wasted.

The only failed Teaching Sprint is one that has not supported teachers to learn about, practise and review a manageable slice of their craft. As you engage in a sequence of Teaching Sprints, you and your colleagues should build capacity to make progressively better, more evidence-informed decisions in the classroom. It won't work neatly every time, because that's the reality of such complex work.

Practitioner Insight

Running Teaching Sprints has shown us there is success and learning in failure. Do we get every Sprint right, every time? We certainly do not, but we do get the opportunity to draw out lessons learned, and that is when the magic happens.

– *Terri Lynn Guimond (principal in Alberta, Canada)*

SUMMARY OF PART 2
The Teaching Sprints Process

- Teaching Sprints is a flexible process for teacher learning and continuous practice improvement.

- Each individual Teaching Sprint consists of three phases: Prepare, Sprint, Review.

- In most settings, teachers can comfortably complete one productive Teaching Sprint in every term of school.

- Each phase of a Teaching Sprint involves a different mode of learning.

- The Prepare Phase enables teams to engage with research evidence, make connections to practice, and define a specific strategy/technique that they would like to trial.

- The Sprint Phase supports teachers to bridge theory and practice; they intentionally practise a selected strategy/technique in classrooms.

- The Review Phase provides the opportunity to reflect on experiences, review impact evidence and determine implications for future practice.

- All phases are supported by simple protocols that teams can use to drive collective thinking and action.

Reflection Activity
Potential Benefits of Teaching Sprints

Consider the positives of using Teaching Sprints for your team or school. Discuss them with your colleagues, and rank the order of potential benefits:

1. Help us to better engage with research evidence about effective teaching

2. Enable us to make better use of collaboration time through structured professional dialogue

3. Provide us with a manageable process for intentionally practising evidence-informed strategies/techniques in the classroom

4. Motivate us to take regular small steps towards enhanced expertise

5. Build psychological safety and a culture of collegial learning

6. Build our sense of collective efficacy – our belief that we can make changes and have a positive impact on student learning

Notes

_____

_____

_____

_____

_____

_____

_____

_____

_____

_____

_____

PART 3

Establishing an Improvement Routine

· ·

I n Part 1, we identified three big ideas that should underscore any practice improvement effort. In Part 2, we detailed a manageable three-step process for engaging in professional learning together. In Part 3, we turn our attention to the practicalities of running Teaching Sprints as an improvement routine.

Making New Habits

Teaching Sprints is designed to become part of the furniture in the regular running of your school. If embedded as an organisational routine, Teaching Sprints should eventually feel habitual. Making a habit of improvement work is the ultimate aim, because habits require minimal energy and motivation to sustain (Duhigg, 2014).

If you take the time to establish a routine for collaborative learning, time becomes your best friend. Over years and years, teachers will cycle through many bursts of hard thinking, practising and reflecting. The resulting small improvements to classroom teaching – sequenced and applied over years – potentially create massive change. By using a habitual system for professional growth, you rely less and less on willpower, motivation and energy to sustain teachers' improvement work.

You may be looking to establish an improvement routine for a *single team* of teachers in a school. Or you may be moving towards embedding a school-wide approach that can support *teams* of teachers. In either case, the ultimate goal is to make an organisational habit of enhancing teachers' expertise.

No Right Way

We think it's important to establish from the outset that there is no one right way to run Teaching Sprints. People all over the world, in diverse educational settings, have used Teaching Sprints to drive practice improvements. In our experience, the teachers, schools and districts that are most successful hold firmly to the intent: every term, teachers come together to learn from the evidence, and they apply their learning incrementally and intentionally. At the same time, these schools adapt the structural elements flexibly: they tweak, stretch, shrink and mold the process itself to fit their team, school or system.

More and more, we see that Teaching Sprints functions best not as a fixed process, but as a guiding framework. It's been designed with enough built-in "wriggle room" for you to make it your own – and in Part 3, we explore how you can do just that.

The Key Questions to Answer

Based on our work in the field, we know there are important practical decisions that need to be made in order to run Teaching Sprints in a school. We consider some of these through three frequently asked questions:

3.1 **Teacher teams:** *Who could work together in Teaching Sprints?*

3.2 **Scheduling:** *When can we run our Teaching Sprints in a busy term?*

3.3 **Focus Area:** *How do we choose an area of practice to work on?*

These are important questions to answer. In our experience, if teachers do not have clarity around these elements, the quality of professional learning may suffer and the likelihood of long-term improvement through the process will be low. Given this, we think it's well worth taking the time to thoughtfully consider these practicalities before you launch into implementation.

3.1 TEACHER TEAMS: WHO COULD WORK TOGETHER IN TEACHING SPRINTS?

Teaching Sprints is designed to support collective efforts. Collaboration is, of course, not an end in itself, but we think it's the means by which teachers can best push their thinking and practice forward in classrooms (Cordingley et al., 2015, p. 7). While Teaching Sprints can support one-to-one instructional coaching, we think it works best in teams of three to eight people.

Teachers can be organised into teams in different ways. Here are some examples:

- Grade- or year-level teams (e.g. Year 1 teachers)

- Faculty/department/domain teams (e.g. Humanities teachers)

- Existing teams (e.g. Professional Learning Community teams)

- Peer coaching triads

- Groups of diverse specialist teachers (e.g. Performing Arts teachers)

- All teachers on staff (in a small rural or remote school)

- Teacher assistants and aides (who may be working on common practice goals)

- Any other variation that reasonably supports teacher learning

In large schools or faculties, there may be existing teams of more than eight people. In these circumstances, you might consider establishing smaller sub-teams or think carefully about how to manage the process best with a larger group.

No matter the structure, there are only two roles to be played in every team: Sprint Leader and Team Member.

Sprint Leader

Each team needs a Sprint Leader. This is the person who will lead the planning and facilitation of every Teaching Sprint. The role of Sprint Leader is usually played by an existing team leader or instructional coach – but any teacher can fulfil this role. In some cases, you may decide that Teaching

Sprints would in fact best be led by someone who is not in a formal position of leadership.

In our experience, most schools choose to assign permanent Sprint Leaders, but you may decide to rotate the role of Sprint Leader so that others have an opportunity to grow their leadership capacity as part of the process. What's most important is that through each and every Teaching Sprint, a leader is designated, visible, proactive and prepared.

Investing in Leaders

Across a school, it is crucial to invest in your current Sprint Leaders. This is often best done by bringing them together on a regular basis to co-plan, share lessons learned and work through implementation questions. It is also useful if current Sprint Leaders can identify and support others who may take on the role over time. This ongoing capacity-building can be helpful for the sustainability of Teaching Sprints in any team, school, or district.

Team Members

The Teaching Sprints approach requires engaged participation from everyone. This is important not just for individual teachers' development, but for building a productive environment in which everyone feels safe to contribute, take risks, challenge ideas and seek feedback.

Table 3.1 offers a simple role summary matched to each of the three phases – Prepare, Sprint and Review.

Table 3.1   The Roles of Sprint Leaders and Team Members

	Sprint Leader	Team Members
Prepare	• Plan the Prepare meeting and identify relevant research evidence to explore • Lead the team members as they engage in new learning about evidence-informed strategies	• Meaningfully engage with relevant research materials • Be open, reflective and proactive in team discussions

	Sprint Leader	Team Members
	• Support the team members as they move through relevant protocols to sharpen their thinking • Help teachers to define and commit to a specific, manageable technique to practise in the Sprint Phase • Schedule the 2–4 week Sprint Phase • Schedule a Check-in meeting (to be held during the Sprint Phase)	• Ask clarifying questions so that you are clear about the focus and confident to proceed to the Sprint Phase • Block out necessary time to practise the agreed technique in the Sprint Phase
Sprint	• Support team members as they implement the Sprint • Plan and run a Check-in meeting • Encourage teachers to collect relevant evidence of impact • Coordinate expert support and instructional guidance where appropriate	• Intentionally practise the agreed practice/strategy • Take note of any barriers to success • Share these at the Check-in meeting • Proactively seek help/clarity from other team members when needed • Seek out (or provide) feedback • Collect relevant evidence of impact throughout the Sprint
Review	• Locate and bring the Review Protocol • Using the reflection questions, facilitate team discussion • Support team members as they share their learning/challenges from the Sprint • Lead a discussion to plan the next steps for professional learning	• Bring any evidence of impact • Be open to sharing your experiences of the Sprint • Consider how you might transfer your new learning into future practice • Share possible next steps for your team's professional learning

Tip From Our Team: Building Psychological Safety

In the process of helping schools to implement Teaching Sprints over several years, it has become apparent that one of the most powerful aspects of Sprints is how it may help support team psychological safety. Team psychological safety underpins team learning. What helps an experienced teacher admit they might have a small gap in teaching expertise? People need to feel they won't be judged or ridiculed for speaking up or contributing in professional dialogue. It can be hard to get beyond a "show and tell" culture, where teachers are collegial but don't necessarily want to risk challenging a peer. The conditions for team psychological safety are facilitated by a team leader who frames the shared work as being about learning, who acknowledges their own fallibility, [who] models how to learn from failure, and who sets norms to build the culture of a team (Edmondson, 2012). Teachers and school leaders have consistently told us that the Teaching Sprints process – with its clear process and protocols – has really helped make a difference to teachers building trust, learning and getting better together.

– Ricky Campbell-Allen (senior faculty, Teaching Sprints)

Facilitating Cross-Team Learning

Because Teaching Sprints are run in teams, there is great potential for cross-team professional learning. If teams are open about what they are focusing on, the sharing of practices can happen quite informally, for example by sharing planning and review notes online (in a shared Google Doc or Microsoft OneNote, for example).

Cross-team learning can also be facilitated more formally. At the end of a series of Teaching Sprints, leaders might run a Sprints Stories session. Here, teams of teachers could come together for short structured presentations (e.g. five minutes per team), to share their experiences around a few key questions:

- What evidence did you engage with in the Prepare Phase? What did you set out to improve?

- How did you implement the strategy in classrooms? What were some of the challenges that emerged?

- What have you learnt about teaching? What would be helpful to share with others looking to pursue improvement in this area?

Scheduling an annual (or semesterly) Sprint Stories session is useful both for building a culture of collaboration, and for highlighting the kinds of research-informed strategies different teams are working on across a school.

Practitioner Insight

Cross-team sharing is so valuable. We use an online platform to share current Sprints, research evidence and impact data. All staff have access to this, which helps keep us on track with Check-ins. It also supports teachers to ask questions and seek further guidance. Using photos and videos of what teachers are trialling has been a great way to document and celebrate collective practice improvements.

– *Leanne McGettigan (principal in Saskatchewan, Canada)*

3.2 SCHEDULING: WHEN CAN WE RUN OUR TEACHING SPRINTS IN A BUSY TERM?

Given the hectic nature of teaching, it makes sense that teachers are drawn to use their collaboration time to complete only the most urgent tasks. If we delay teacher learning in favour of curriculum planning or administrative tasks in any given meeting, we will probably barely notice. But if we make a habit of this, we might drift for whole terms (or years), working hard without ever systematically and intentionally getting better at what we do. Scheduling and *protecting* specific slices of time for Teaching Sprints is essential.

What Meetings Do We Need to Schedule?

As teams of teachers move through a Teaching Sprint, they need scheduled time for at least three meetings. This is flexible, but we recommend the following meeting lengths as a guide:

Prepare	Sprint	Review
One 90-minute meeting *or* Two 60-minute meetings	One 15-minute Check-in	One 45-minute meeting

Identifying Existing Blocks of Time

The best way to schedule Teaching Sprints in a school term is to first complete an exhaustive audit of the existing allocated collaboration time. Map out the blocks of time that are currently scheduled for both full staff and specific team meetings. Be sure to include staff meetings, briefings, whole-school staff development days, grade and faculty meetings, Professional Learning Communities, and so on. Include duration details, so that you know how much time is allocated to each activity in every school term. For example, you might list the following:

Whole staff development day: 5 hours, once a term (5 hours per term)

Team meetings: 1.5 hours, twice a term (3 hours per term)

Whole staff weekly briefings: 30 minutes, eight times a term (4 hours per term)

As you go, you might like to quickly rate the effectiveness (on a scale) of these collaborative activities in enhancing teachers' expertise (for example, 1 = ineffective for developing expertise, 5 = highly effective for developing expertise). Don't worry about being exact in your judgments here, but take the opportunity to roughly determine which meetings are currently effective for building teacher capacity across the school year.

Reallocating Time

Once you have canvassed the blocks of time, you can consider which might be reallocated to the Teaching Sprints process. The key is to demarcate specific periods of time for the Sprints meetings listed above, because it won't be enough to simply suggest that, at some point, teachers need to squeeze these into a jam-packed existing schedule.

Remember that everyone is busy. We will *all* naturally put off professional learning for something more urgent. Scheduling Teaching Sprints properly makes it as easy as possible for teachers to sustain the challenging work of developing their craft.

To support your analysis of existing collaboration time, you might like to use the template in Appendix H, "Reallocating Time for Teaching Sprints".

Scheduling Options

Teaching Sprints can be scheduled in many different ways. Below are some examples from the field which we hope will stimulate thinking for your own planning.

How You Might Schedule the Prepare Meeting/s

- Reallocate one 60-to-90-minute session on a full staff development day. All staff might be located in the same space, but they sit and work in teams to prepare their next term's Teaching Sprint.
- Run a twilight after-school session (including afternoon tea) from 3.30 p.m. to 5.00 p.m.
- Schedule one extended 90-minute Professional Learning Community (PLC) meeting early in the term.
- Senior leaders take students for a 60-minute assembly early in the term to free up a few teams of teachers.

How You Might Schedule the Check-in Meeting (During the Sprint Phase)

- The principal gives the first 15 minutes of a full staff meeting for teams to meet for their Check-in.
- Grade or faculty teams assign the first agenda item of an existing meeting to run the Check-in.
- The first 15 minutes of a regular PLC meeting is allocated to the Check-in.
- Teams find a time before or after school on a set day of each term to run the Check-in.

How You Might Schedule the Review Meeting

- Allocate one 60-minute PLC or grade/faculty meeting late in the term.
- Run a 45-minute before-school session (this could be done with all staff together, seated in teams).
- Allocate one whole staff meeting for every team to run their Review meeting.

To support your planning of the required meetings, you might like to use the Teaching Sprints Term Planner (see Appendix I).

Practitioner Insights: Scheduling Time for Teaching Sprints

What we spend most of our time on usually shows staff what we value most. As [leaders] of learning, we want the focus on just that. Many traditional staff meetings can be replaced by simply sending an email or by running a quick meeting at the end of a Check-in. We start by scheduling professional learning time for staff and *then* we schedule other necessary meetings for administration. By prioritising teacher learning in the schedule, we show what is valued in our school.

– Leanne McGettigan (principal in Saskatchewan, Canada)

To move Teaching Sprints beyond the "coalition of the willing", you need to ensure that schools have a firm structure of embedded time dedicated to the process and that the principal is invested in its potential success. In short, ensure your principal honours the process and the time for staff to engage in it.

– Kristie O'Neill (professional learning coordinator in New South Wales, Australia)

To truly leverage Teaching Sprints, it is important for school leadership to find ways to embed time within teachers' daily schedules. During early implementation, this was the most consistent feedback we received. Time is a precious gift. When teachers are freed up to meet without having to prep or plan for students, it provides opportunity for administrators to support the work. It shows that school leaders value (and are invested in) the process.

– Terri Lynn Guimond (principal in Alberta, Canada)

Extending the Prepare Phase

Sometimes teachers go digging into particularly challenging areas of practice; knowledge-building in the Prepare Phase can be involved work. In some cases, teams might decide to extend the Prepare Phase beyond one or two meetings. We've spoken to many teachers who've said they wanted more time to build a stronger knowledge base before committing to action in the Sprint Phase. Although we encourage a bias towards action, we agree it's important that practice is built on robust understanding. In our experience, teachers are well-placed to judge what they need, so we encourage flexibility here.

Following an extended Prepare Phase, it's of course still crucial to move into intentional practice and reflection through the Sprint and Review Phases. While the front end of the process may be extended, every Teaching Sprint (as a whole) should retain a sense of momentum.

Gathering Feedback to Refine Your Schedule

As you implement Sprints in your context, it's crucial to seek regular and honest feedback from teachers. One way to do this is to use the Teaching Sprints Pulse Check Survey, a simple tool for collecting anonymous feedback from teams. In our experience, most team or school leaders find it useful to seek and review feedback every 6 to 12 months. Remember that there is no "right way" to schedule Teaching Sprints, so it's helpful to be responsive to teachers and iterative in implementation.

Go to https://teachingsprints.com/survey to download the survey.

3.3 FOCUS AREA: HOW DO WE CHOOSE AN AREA OF PRACTICE TO WORK ON?

Selecting a Focus

In theory, we can all be running Teaching Sprints on different aspects of teaching, but it's helpful to choose a broad practice area in which teachers can enhance their expertise.

Many teachers will have experienced professional learning that runs a mile wide and an inch deep; it's frustrating to teachers when the focus for practice improvement chops and changes before meaningful progress can be made. Given the critically limited time teachers have, and the inherent complexities of building expertise, we suggest that teams *stay the course* with one broad focus over multiple Teaching Sprints. This might mean choosing and setting a focus for 6, 9, 18 or 24 months; the point is that all teachers need sufficient time to learn about and develop new habits of practice (Cordingley et al., 2015; Wiliam, 2016).

Wherever possible, we advocate setting a common (e.g. school-wide) focus for Teaching Sprints. This promotes collaboration, builds collective expertise in a given area, and enables more efficient sharing of research and resources across teams. Of course, the specific aims of different teams and teachers may differ, and it's important to factor in domain-specific adjustments. But setting a broad focus provides helpful common boundaries around what staff, in any given school or team, could work on next.

Approaches to Setting a Focus

You can use Teaching Sprints to develop almost any aspect of practice. But as we argued in Part 1, we don't think we should indulge in developing any and all teaching strategies, because the danger of basing professional learning on approaches with weak evidence is clear: teachers might become more fluent in implementing techniques that are not themselves optimal. We think it makes sense to prioritise *only* those practices for which there is good evidence of a likely high pay-off for students.

There are four approaches that teams and schools typically take to select a focus for their Teaching Sprints:

1. Use Teaching Sprints Starters.

2. Use a research-based, practice-focused book.

3. Use resources from the Teaching Sprints Research Hub.

4. Use school or system resources.

1. Using Teaching Sprints Starters

There is an emerging consensus about the effectiveness of a small set of techniques that can be used in the teaching of all subjects, and with students of varying ages. Sometimes called high-leverage or high-impact teaching strategies, these are approaches that most (if not all) teachers can meaningfully develop. We've gathered together a set of these strategies because we think they are helpful if you're just getting going with Teaching Sprints – we call them the Teaching Sprints Starters.

Most of the starters will be familiar to teachers. The strategies are relatively easy to isolate for intentional practice, and they are gathered from a range of evidence-informed, teacher-friendly sources (see Figure 3.1 on page 55). In our experience, all teachers (no matter their existing level of expertise) can benefit from improving how and when they use these techniques in the classroom.

For everything you need to get going with the Teaching Sprints Starters, head to https://teachingsprints.com/starters.

Teaching Sprints Starters

Starters for Giving Clear and Precise Explanations

To build expertise in giving clear and precise explanations, your team might run a Teaching Sprint on one of the following principles/techniques:

Teaching Sprints Starters: The Teaching Sprints Starters take you right to an evidence-informed technique to be practised in the Sprint. Organised under broad elements of practice, they are available for you to explore at http://www.teachingsprints.com/starters.

- Present material in small steps (Rosenshine, 2012).

- Use fully worked examples (Rosenshine, 2012).

- Use concrete examples for abstract concepts (Learning Scientists, n.d.).

- Model metacognitive talk (EEF, 2018).

Starters for Regularly Checking for Understanding

To build expertise in checking for student understanding, your team might run a Teaching Sprint on one of the following principles/techniques:

- Check responses of all students – for example, on mini whiteboards (Rosenshine, 2012).

- Pick non-volunteers or "Cold call" (Lemov, 2015, or see Sherrington, 2020).

- Ask multiple-choice questions and use A, B, C, D flashcards (Wiliam, 2018, p. 105).

Starters for Embedding Different
Kinds of Practice in Instruction

To build expertise in engaging students in different forms of practice, your team might run a Teaching Sprint on one of the following principles/ techniques:

- Embed opportunities for retrieval practice (Learning Scientists, n.d.).

- Space the revision of concepts (Science of Learning Research Centre, 2014–2020).

- Move students through phases of guided practice (Rosenshine, 2012).

- Mix up practice tasks to boost performance (Science of Learning Research Centre, 2014–2020).

Starters for Encouraging Accuracy,
Precision and Depth of Student Response

To build expertise in setting high expectations for academic engagement, your team might run a Teaching Sprint on one of the following principles/ techniques:

- Set high expectations for accuracy or "Right is right" (Lemov, 2015).

- Add nuance or depth to responses (Sumeracki, 2020).

- Ask students to re-state responses for accuracy or "Say it again better" (Lemov, 2015 or see Sherrington, 2018).

Starters for Building Students' Conceptions of "Quality"

To build expertise in communicating conceptions of quality to students, your team might run a Teaching Sprint on one of the following principles/ techniques:

- Start with samples of work to communicate quality (LSI Dylan Wiliam Center, 2015).

- Provide opportunities for students to compare and discuss conceptions of quality or "Choose, swap, choose" (Wiliam, 2018, p. 80).

- Facilitate the exchange of positive and critical peer feedback or "Two stars and a wish" (LSI Dylan Wiliam Center, 2015 or Wiliam, 2018, p. 161).

Figure 3.1   Open-Source Materials Used for the Teaching Sprints Starters

- The Learning Scientists' Six Strategies for Effective Learning: https://www.learningscientists.org/downloadable-materials

- Education Endowment Foundation Guidance Reports: https://education endowmentfoundation.org.uk/tools/guidance-reports

- LSI Dylan Wiliam Center: https://www.dylanwiliamcenter.com

- Barak Rosenshine's "Principles of Instruction: Research-Based Strategies That All Teachers Should Know": https://aft.org/sites/default/files/periodi cals/Rosenshine.pdf

- Former Headteacher Tom Sherrington's *Teacherhead* blog: https://teacher head.com

- Science of Learning Research Centre's PEN Principles: https://slrc.org .au/resources/pen-principles

- Doug Lemov and Uncommon Schools' Teach Like a Champion: teachlikea champion.com

Working on Generic Techniques in a Subject Area or Domain

Though high-leverage strategies are generally described, the techniques are always implemented in a domain, subject or content area; they cannot be trialled or practised in a vacuum. If you want to improve your capacity to give precise explanations, you would work on this in a specific content area; science teachers, for example, may want to improve the way they explain the layout of the periodic table or the functions of the cardiovascular system. It's critical to acknowledge that the effectiveness of the implementation of these techniques will always be at least partly dependent on teachers' depth of content knowledge.

Famously highlighted by Lee Shulman (1986, 1987), subject content knowledge is critically important for teachers. Professor Rob Coe and colleagues provide a helpful top-line summary of the importance of this knowledge in good practice (Coe et al., 2020, p. 20):

> Great teachers understand the content they are teaching and how it is learnt. This means they should have deep and fluent knowledge and flexible understanding of the content they are teaching and how it is learnt, including its inherent dependencies. They should have an explicit repertoire of well-crafted explanations, examples and tasks for each topic they teach.

So, content knowledge matters. It's important to understand that to maximise efforts with the Teaching Sprints Starters (or any other generic strategies), teachers will sometimes need time to first strengthen elements of their content knowledge. Downplaying or ignoring the role of domain-specific knowledge can be detrimental to efforts to improve teacher practice.

2. Using a Research-Based, Practice-Focused Book

Some schools and teams prefer to drive their Teaching Sprints work through a book. While this is invariably more costly than using open-source materials, we think it's a great way to establish a common agenda for medium-to-long-term practice improvement.

There are a few books which we think pair particularly well with the Teaching Sprints approach.

Recommended Books for Teaching Sprints

Understanding How We Learn (Weinstein & Sumeracki, 2018)

This guide outlines the key findings from cognitive science most relevant to teaching. It provides a clear and practical introduction to spaced practice, retrieval practice, interleaving, elaboration, concrete examples and dual coding.

Rosenshine's Principles in Action (Sherrington, 2019)

Barak Rosenshine's Principles of Instruction provide teachers with the "core ingredients" of effective, explicit instruction. In this book, Tom Sherrington expands on Rosenshine's original paper, neatly reorganising the principles into strands and offering specific examples of the principles "in action". This is great material for a sequence of Teaching Sprints focused on aspects of explicit instruction.

Embedded Formative Assessment (2nd ed.) (Wiliam, 2018)

Dylan Wiliam presents a compelling argument for focusing improvement efforts on formative assessment before laying out specific techniques all teachers can trial. *Embedded Formative Assessment* would make a great basis for a series of Teaching Sprints on short-cycle formative assessment.

Teaching Walkthrus (Sherrington & Caviglioli, 2020)

This highly practical guide describes, organises and depicts various evidence-informed teaching techniques. *Teaching Walkthrus* does a lot of hard work to bridge theory and practice for teachers, and we think it gets right to a useful "grain size" for Teaching Sprints.

Powerful Teaching (Agarwal & Bain, 2019)

This book supports teachers to think critically about existing teaching practice in light of current cognitive science research. This resource is teacher-friendly and could support a sequence of Teaching Sprints exploring the science of learning in any teacher's classroom.

Responsive Teaching (Fletcher-Wood, 2018)

Structured around six questions familiar to all teachers, this book is a useful guide to cognitive science and formative assessment in the classroom. Fletcher-Wood outlines important principles of responsive teaching and lays out the resources that are most relevant for teachers' work in this area.

Practitioner Insight: Using a Book to Drive Teaching Sprints

We used *Rosenshine's Principles in Action* by Tom Sherrington as the basis for our Teaching Sprints work. Each team member read a principle and gave feedback to the group about what it entailed. From there, we chose one principle to focus on, always developing

(Continued)

(Continued)

something relevant to us and the content we were going to teach. Term after term, we enhanced practice around a different principle. In theory, this one book provides almost three years' worth of material for Teaching Sprints!

– Natalie Dolan (teacher in New South Wales, Australia)

3. Using Resources From the Teaching Sprint Research Hub

To explore a broader set of resources, some teams start at our Teaching Sprints Research Hub (https://teachingsprints.com/research). Here, you can find a carefully curated list of quality open-source materials that we think make useful inputs for a Teaching Sprint.

At the Research Hub, you'll find resources to support teacher learning in these areas:

- Formative assessment

- Feedback strategies

- Retrieval practice and spaced review

- Cognitive load theory

- Metacognition and self-regulation

- Literacy

- Numeracy

Focusing on Literacy and Numeracy

Many schools have used Teaching Sprints to build expertise in teaching literacy and numeracy; we know that some have had particular success with an explicit focus on improving vocabulary instruction. Depending on the aims of your school or team, the Teaching Sprints process alone is not always sufficient to build the kind of expertise teachers need in these domains.

For professional learning in literacy and numeracy, we recommend a significant focus on building content knowledge; lengthening the Prepare Phase (to two or three meetings, spread out over a term) is one way to adapt the process in order for teachers to more meaningfully grapple with the best available research. We also recommend the active engagement of domain-specific instructional coaches/experts. In the Sprint Phase, this could involve internal or external experts observing teachers and offering domain-specific feedback. In the Review Phase, it could involve instructional coaches coming together with teams of teachers to review progress and support the planning of next steps.

However you approach professional learning in literacy and numeracy, the point is to be wary of launching too quickly into practising techniques before doing the necessary knowledge-building. To get you started, we have collected some high-quality literacy and numeracy resources on the Teaching Sprints Research Hub. We hope they're helpful if you're looking for evidence-informed inputs for your work in these critically important domains.

4. Using School or System Resources

Many schools and school systems already have a well-established focus for professional learning; some schools will already use a particular instructional model or set of teaching principles. These may be the most appropriate inputs for your practice improvement work.

Teaching Sprints is not designed to be a "new thing" for your school to learn. It's designed to open the door for all educators, in every school term of every year, to access research evidence in a way that meaningfully encourages learning. If you have an established and evidence-informed focus for improvement work already, we recommend you use this as the basis for your teachers' professional development.

Considering a Teaching Sprints Research Lead

Making sense of research isn't always easy; it takes time. So, depending on the resources you're using, it can be helpful to have a designated member of staff do some of the "legwork" for teams.

Inspired by the role of school "Research Lead" advocated by ResearchED and the Education Development Trust (Bennett, 2016), many schools are embracing the role of a Teaching Sprints Research Lead. Though the specifics of the role may vary, this person typically allocates some time to reviewing and summarising relevant research with (or for) teams.

Practitioner Insight – Research Lead

In the role of Teaching Sprints Research Lead, I've been able to actively and directly support our teachers' improvement work. In the short term, I have gathered and interpreted research to inform Teaching Sprints across the school. In the long term, I want to effect cultural change so that good research evidence is at the heart of all pedagogy at our school.

– Annabelle Marinelli (Teaching Sprints
Research Lead in Victoria, Australia)

SUMMARY OF PART 3
Establishing an Improvement Routine

- Teaching Sprints is designed to make improvement work habitual in your school

- The composition of teams in Teaching Sprints is flexible but we recommend running Sprints with teams of three to eight people

- There are only two roles to be played in every team – Sprint Leader and Team Member

- A review of your existing meeting schedule can be used to identify potential blocks of time that can be reallocated for Teaching Sprints

- For each Teaching Sprint, teams need the time for a Prepare meeting, a Check-in, and a Review meeting

- Setting a school-wide focus for Teaching Sprints can promote the efficient sharing of evidence and resources

- What's most important is that Teaching Sprints works for you in your context – adapt it flexibly and thoughtfully for your team or school

Reflection Activity
Making It Work in Your Team, School or System

Part 3 was organised around three frequently asked implementation questions:

- **3.1 Teacher teams:** *Who could work together in Teaching Sprints?*

- **3.2 Scheduling:** *When can we run our Teaching Sprints in a busy term?*

- **3.3 Focus Area:** *How do we choose an area of practice to work on?*

Drawing on what you know about your context, we now invite you to start a conversation with colleagues or leaders about how Teaching Sprints might work best for you. Take notes as you explore options with your peers.

Teacher teams – *In your context, what sort of team compositions could work well?*

_____

_____

_____

Scheduling – *Considering your analysis of existing collaboration time (Appendix H), when could you schedule Teaching Sprints in the school term?*

_____

_____

_____

Focus Area – *Given your goals and strategic priorities, what kind of focus would make sense for your work in Teaching Sprints?*

_____

_____

_____

Conclusion

Better Than Before

"Better is possible. It does not take genius. It takes diligence. It takes moral clarity. It takes ingenuity. And above all, it takes a willingness to try." (Gawande, 2007, p. 246)

In this book, we've outlined a set of ideas and a simple process designed to support all teachers to get better at what they do best. Like a good cover band, you need to feel comfortable putting your own riff or style on the Teaching Sprints approach; equally, we hope you can avoid making a "terminal mutation" along the way. We encourage you to stay true to the underlying aims, principles and intent of the process – it's about incremental evidence-informed improvement, it's about intentional practice in classrooms, and it's about getting better together.

Our great hope is that Teaching Sprints can come to life in your school or across your system, providing you with a powerful organisational routine that can sustain momentum for professional growth over time.

Whether you're a classroom teacher thinking about your own goals, an instructional leader supporting colleagues to teach better tomorrow, or a school leader interested in redesigning your program for professional learning, we hope you've taken something helpful from this book.

Participating in Our Community

Join the Teaching Sprints community. As we said at the beginning, Teaching Sprints is our collective answer to the challenge of school-based professional learning, but it's just the starting point. Thousands of teachers have engaged with the process; teachers and leaders around the world are considering how to make Sprints work best in their contexts. As you've read this book, you've no doubt already been thinking about what this might look like in your patch. We would love to hear from you.

We invite you to join our community through the Teaching Sprints website, online academy and social media accounts. Feel free to share examples of how you are using the process in your school. Your insights will help us shape the future of Teaching Sprints.

Please go to https://www.teachingsprints.com to connect, take inspiration, and share experiences of getting better together.

Appendices

Appendix A – Teaching Sprints Process Overview

Prepare

Come together to determine a focus for practice improvement

In this phase, teachers:

- Engage in new learning, informed by research evidence
- Draw out connections and challenges to practice
- Determine a precise strategy/technique for practice improvement

Sprint

Intentionally practise in classrooms

Over 2 to 4 weeks, teachers:

- Intentionally practise the chosen strategy/technique in classrooms
- Make adjustments, in light of what's happening
- Check in with colleagues to sustain momentum

Review

Reflect on the process and learn from each other

In this phase, teachers:

- Reflect on the effectiveness of the Sprint
- Share insights and determine implications for future practice
- Identify possible next steps for professional learning

Appendix B – Research Jigsaw Protocol

This protocol supports individual teachers to make sense of small excerpts of research.

Assign team members to read or access parts of research, then share findings and make sense of new learning together.

Name of team member	Resource (or chapter/section)	Summary of key concepts/ideas
1		
2		
3		
4		
5		

Appendix C – Learn & Let Go Protocol

Sometimes, to embrace new evidence-informed approaches, we need to let go of existing practices.

Learn

What have we learnt from the evidence about effective teaching?

Let Go

In light of this, what existing practices may need to be adjusted or retired?

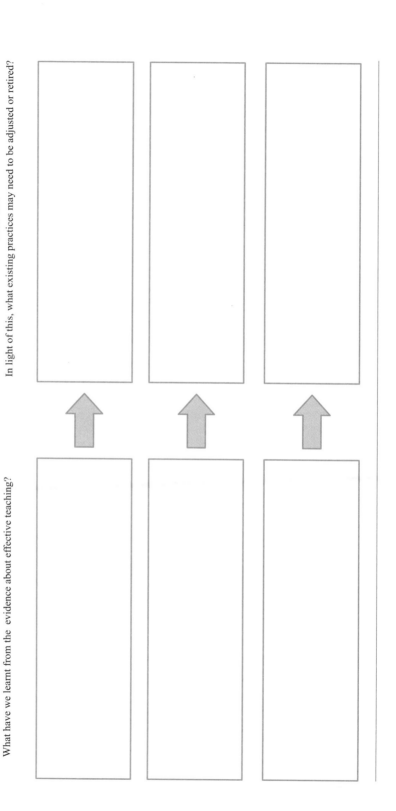

Appendix D – Boulder, Pebble, Sand Protocol

This protocol supports teachers to narrow their focus for practice improvement.

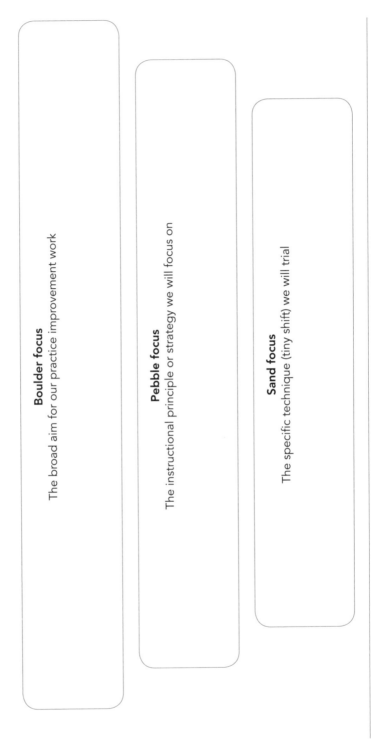

Boulder focus

The broad aim for our practice improvement work

Pebble focus

The instructional principle or strategy we will focus on

Sand focus

The specific technique (tiny shift) we will trial

Appendix E – Picture of Practice Protocol

This protocol supports teachers to get precise about what an agreed practice change will really look like in the classroom.

What would it look like?

With precision, describe (or draw) the changes to teacher behaviour you expect to see. What will you be doing or saying that would show adoption of the new strategy or technique?

Technique
Technique you are going to trial in the Sprint

Appendix F – Check-in Protocol

The Check-in Protocol helps the team to:

1. *Sustain motivation.* The check-in provides a little 'nudge' to support teachers to follow through on the changes they have committed to trialling in their classrooms.

2. *Encourage adjustment.* Sometimes elements of the Sprint need to be refined after teachers have made a start in their own classrooms. The check-in provides time to identify challenges and 'tweak' as needed.

3. *Provide supports.* The check-in gives a structured format for teachers to ask for additional help or resources in order to build their capacity throughout the Sprint.

Protocol Set-Up

Set a 15-minute timer on your phone.

Group stands in a circle.

The key questions that drive the Check-in Protocol:

Done
How are we progressing with the new strategy/technique?

Stuck
Is anybody stuck?
Does anyone need resources or support?

Tweak
What adjustments can we make in order to increase the effectiveness of the Sprint?

Set-Up

Suggested Meeting Time: 45–60 minutes

Materials: Any impact evidence relevant to the Sprint

What happened?

Q1. What was our experience of the Sprint?

- What did we actually practise in our teaching?
- How do we feel about it? In what ways do we think we have improved in the focus area?
- What did we notice ourselves needing to unlearn (or adjust), in order to build fluency with the new technique?

Q2. What can we reasonably conclude from the impact evidence we have?

- What do we think was the impact of the Sprint? What can the evidence tell us, and what does it suggest about potential long-term impacts?
- Which students seemed to benefit most from the change to practice? Why do we think that might be the case?

Where to next?

Q3. What are the implications for practice?

- How might we continue to make a habit of using this strategy?
- How can we apply what we've learnt more broadly in our teaching?

Q4. What are the next steps for our professional learning?

- What would be the best next step to take to consolidate our learning?
- What do we want to know more about? What emerging questions do we have?
- Which sources of research evidence could we explore further?

Appendix H – Reallocating Time for Teaching Sprints

Step 1: Outline all significant staff and team collaboration time (e.g. whole staff meetings or Professional Learning Communities).

Step 2: Record the total duration of each collaborative activity over a school term (e.g. 5 hours per term).

Step 3: Discuss the impact of each activity on professional practice, and determine what time in a term may be reallocated to Teaching Sprints.

Suggested rating scale: 1 = Ineffective for developing expertise; 5 = Highly effective for developing expertise

Staff and Team Collaboration Activity	Duration	Impact on Practice	Reallocation
What is the activity? Who is involved?	How long is allocated for this across a term?	What has been the impact on practice? Use a simple rating, e.g. 1–5	How might you reallocate some of this time to Teaching Sprints?

Appendix I – Teaching Sprints Term Planner

Prepare Phase: Schedule one or two meetings for your Prepare Phase. We recommend you schedule this early in the term.

Sprint Phase: Determine a period of 2–4 weeks for the Sprint Phase. In that time, schedule one 15-minute Check-in meeting.

Review Phase: After the Sprint Phase, schedule one Review meeting.

			Week of School Term								
	1	2	3	4	5	6	7	8	9	10
Prepare Phase Schedule one 90-minute meeting or two 60-minute meetings.										
Sprint Phase Allocate 2–4 weeks for the Sprint. Schedule one 15-minute Check-in meeting.										
Review Phase Schedule one 45- or 60-minute meeting.										

References

Agarwal, P. K., & Bain, P. M. (2019). *Powerful teaching: Unleash the science of learning*. John Wiley & Sons.

Bell, M., Cordingley, P., Isham, C., & Davis, R. (2010). Report of professional practitioner use of research review: Practitioner engagement in and/or with research. CUREE, GTCE, LSIS and NTRP.

Bennett, T. (2016). *The school Research Lead*. Education Development Trust. https://www.educationdevelopmenttrust.com/Education DevelopmentTrust/files/93/93c332a4-40df-41ac-8a9b-f803c6573d10 .pdf

Berliner, D. C. (1986). In pursuit of the expert pedagogue. *Educational Researcher*, *15*(7), 5–13. https://doi.org/10.3102/0013189X015007007

Berliner, D. C. (2004). Describing the behavior and documenting the accomplishments of expert teachers. *Bulletin of Science, Technology & Society*, *24*(3), 200–212. https://doi.org/10.1177/0270467604265535

Campbell, C., Lieberman, A., & Yashkina, A. (2016). Developing professional capital in policy and practice: Ontario's Teacher Learning and Leadership Program. *Journal of Professional Capital and Community*, *1*(3), 219–236. https://doi.org/10.1108/JPCC-03-2016-0004

Clear, J. (2018). *Atomic habits: An easy & proven way to build good habits & break bad ones*. Penguin Publishing Group.

Coe, R., & Kime, S. (2019). *A (new) manifesto for evidence-based education: Twenty years on*. Evidence Based Education. https://evidence based.education/new-manifesto-evidence-based-education

Coe, R., Rauch, C. J., Kime, S., & Singleton, D. (2020). *The Great Teaching Toolkit evidence review*. Evidence Based Education. www .greatteaching.com

Cohen, D. K. (2011). *Teaching and its predicaments*. Harvard University Press.

Cole, P. (2012). Linking effective professional learning with effective teaching practice. Australian Institute for Teaching and School Leadership.

Colvin, G. (2019). *Talent is overrated: What really separates world-class performers from everybody else.* Hachette, UK.

Cordingley, P. (2015). The contribution of research to teachers' professional learning and development. *Oxford Review of Education, 41*(2), 234–252.

Cordingley, P., Bell, M., Thomason, S., & Firth, A. (2005). The impact of collaborative CPD on classroom teaching and learning. Review: How do collaborative and sustained CPD and sustained but not collaborative CPD affect teaching and learning. Social Science Research Unit, Institute of Education, University of London. http://eppi.ioe.ac.uk/cms/Default.aspx

Cordingley, P., Higgins, S., Greany, T., Buckler, N., Coles-Jordan, D., Crisp, B., Saunders, L., & Coe, R. (2015). *Developing great teaching: Lessons from the international reviews into effective professional development.* Teacher Development Trust. http://tdtrust.org/about/dgt

Deans for Impact. (2016). *Practice with purpose: The emerging science of teacher expertise.* Deans for Impact. https://deansforimpact.org/wp-content/uploads/2016/12/Practice-with-Purpose_FOR-PRINT_113016.pdf

Duhigg, C. (2014). *The power of habit: Why we do what we do in life and business* (Random House Trade Paperback ed.). Random House.

Edmondson, A. C. (2012). *Teaming: How organizations learn, innovate, and compete in the knowledge economy.* John Wiley & Sons.

Education Endowment Foundation. (2018, April 27). Metacognition and self-regulated learning. Education Endowment Foundation. https://educationendowmentfoundation.org.uk/tools/guidance-reports/metacognition-and-self-regulated-learning

Education Endowment Foundation. (2020). *Practical tools.* Education Endowment Foundation. https://educationendowmentfoundation.org.uk/tools

Education Hub. (2020). *The Education Hub.* https://theeducationhub.org.nz

Ericsson, K. A. (2006). The influence of experience and deliberate practice on the development of superior expert performance. In K. A. Ericsson, N. Charness, P. J. Feltovich, & R. R. Hoffman (Eds.), *The Cambridge handbook of expertise and expert performance* (pp. 683–704). Cambridge University Press. https://doi.org/10.1017/CBO9780511816796.038

Ericsson, K. A. (2008). Deliberate practice and acquisition of expert performance: A general overview. *Academic Emergency Medicine, 15*(11), 988–994. https://doi.org/10.1111/j.1553-2712.2008.00227

Ericsson, K. A. (2016). *Peak: Secrets from the new science of expertise.* Houghton Mifflin Harcourt.

Ericsson, K. A., & Harwell, K. W. (2019). Deliberate practice and proposed limits on the effects of practice on the acquisition of expert performance: Why the original definition matters and recommendations for future research. *Frontiers in Psychology, 10,* 2396. https://doi.org/10.3389/fpsyg.2019.02396

Ericsson, K. A., Hoffman, R. R., Kozbelt, A., & Williams, A. M. (Eds.). (2018). *The Cambridge handbook of expertise and expert performance* (2nd ed.). Cambridge University Press.

Ericsson, K. A., Krampe, R. T., & Tesch-Romer, C. (1993). The role of deliberate practice in the acquisition of expert performance. *Psychological Review, 100,* 363.

Evidence for Learning. (n.d.). Retrieved January 2, 2020, from https://evidenceforlearning.org.au

Fletcher-Wood, H. (2018). *Responsive teaching: Cognitive science and formative assessment in practice.* Routledge.

Fogg, B. J. (2020). *Tiny habits: The small changes that change everything.* Houghton Mifflin Harcourt.

Gawande, A. (2007). *Better: A surgeon's notes on performance.* Metropolitan.

Hargreaves, A., & O'Connor, M. T. (2018). *Collaborative professionalism: When teaching together means learning for all.* Corwin.

Hatano, G., & Inagaki, T. (1986). Two courses of expertise. In H. Stevenson, H. Azuma, & K. Hakuta (Eds.), *Child development and education in Japan* (pp. 262–272). W. H. Freeman.

Harris, A., Jones, M., & Huffman, J. (Eds.). (2017). *Teachers leading educational reform: The power of professional learning communities.* Routledge.

Hattie, J. (2003, October). *Teachers make a difference: What is the research evidence?* Paper presented at the Australian Council for

Educational Research Conference, Melbourne. http://research.acer
.edu.au/research_conference_2003/4

Heath, D., & Heath, C. (2011). *Switch: How to change things when change is hard*. Random House.

Jones, K. (2020). *Retrieval practice: Resources and research for every classroom*. John Catt Educational Ltd.

Kennedy, M. M. (2016). How does professional development improve teaching? *Review of Educational Research, 86*(4), 945–980. https://doi.org/10.3102/0034654315626800

Kirschner, P. A., & Hendrick, C. (2020). *How learning happens: Seminal works in educational psychology and what they mean in practice*. Routledge.

Learning Scientists. (n.d.). Downloadable materials. *The Learning Scientists*. https://www.learningscientists.org/downloadable-materials

Le Fevre, D., Timperley, H., & Ell, F. (2016). Curriculum and pedagogy: The future of teacher professional learning and the development of adaptive expertise. In D. Wyse, L. Hayward, & J. Pandya (Eds.), *The SAGE handbook of curriculum, pedagogy and assessment* (Vol. 2, pp. 309–324). SAGE Publications Ltd.

Lemov, D. (2015). *Teach like a champion 2.0: 62 techniques that put students on the path to college*. Jossey-Bass.

Lemov, D., Woolway, E., & Yezzi, K. (2018). *Practice perfect: 42 rules for getting better at getting better*. John Wiley & Sons.

LSI Dylan Wiliam Center. (2015, February 3). Practical ideas for classroom formative assessment. *LSI Dylan Wiliam Center*. https://www.dylanwiliamcenter.com/2015/02/03/practical-ideas-for-classroom-formative-assessment

Mccrea, P. (2018). *Expert teaching: What is it, and how might we develop it?* Institute for Teaching. https://s3.eu-west-2.amazonaws.com/ambition-institute/documents/What_is_Expert_Teaching_-_Peps_Mccrea_1.pdf

Nelson, J., & Walker, M. (2019, May 19). Evidence-informed approaches to teaching – Where are we now? *The NFER Blog*. https://www.nfer.ac.uk/news-events/nfer-blogs/evidence-informed-approaches-to-teaching-where-are-we-now

Quigley, A. (2013, April 11). Overcoming the ok plateau: How to go beyond satisfactory and become an expert teacher. *The Guardian*.

https://www.theguardian.com/teacher-network/teacher-blog/2013/apr/11/expert-teachers-ok-plateau-professional-development

ResearchED. (n.d.). *Our story – ResearchED*. Retrieved July 29, 2020, from https://researched.org.uk/about/our-story

Rice, J. (2013). Learning from experience? Evidence on the impact and distribution of teacher experience and the implications for teacher policy. *Education Finance and Policy*, *8*(3), 332–348.

Rivkin, S. G., Hanushek, E. A., & Kain, J. F. (2005). Teachers, schools, and academic achievement. *Econometrica*, *73*(2), 417–458.

Rosenshine, B. (2012, Spring). Principles of instruction: Research-based strategies that all teachers should know. *American Educator*, 12–19, 39. https://aft.org/sites/default/files/periodicals/Rosenshine.pdf

Science of Learning Research Centre. (2014–2020). Science of Learning Research Centre PEN Principles. https://slrc.org.au/resources/pen-principles

Sharples, J. (2013). *Evidence for the frontline*. Alliance for Useful Evidence.

Sharples, J. (2017, December 1). *EEF Blog: Untangling the "Literacy Octopus" – three crucial lessons from the latest EEF evaluation | News*. https://educationendowmentfoundation.org.uk/news/untangling-the-literacy-octopus

Sherrington, T. (2018). Great teaching: The power of questioning. https://teacherhead.com/2018/08/24/great-teaching-the-power-of-questioning/

Sherrington, T. (2019). *Rosenshine's principles in action*. John Catt Educational Ltd.

Sherrington, T. (2020). Top Three! High-impact, inclusive questioning strategies. https://teacherhead.com/2020/09/14/top-three-high-impact-inclusive-questioning-strategies/comment-page-1/

Sherrington, T., & Caviglioli, O. (2020). *Teaching walkthrus: Visual step-by-step guides to essential teaching techniques*. John Catt Educational Ltd.

Shulman, L. S. (1986). Those who understand: Knowledge growth in teaching. *Educational Researcher*, *15*(20), 4–14.

Shulman, L. S. (1987). Knowledge and teaching: Foundations of the New Reform. *Harvard Educational Review*, *57*(1), 1–22.

Sumeracki, M. (2020, February 20). Elaboration as self-explanation. *The Learning Scientists*. https://www.learningscientists.org/blog/2020/2/20-1

Sutton Trust. (2020). *Our research*. Sutton Trust. https://www.suttontrust.com/our-research

Thaler, R. H., & Sunstein, C. R. (2009). *Nudge: Improving decisions about health, wealth, and happiness*. Penguin.

Timperley, H. (2008). *Teacher professional learning and development*. The Educational Practices Series – 18 Ed. Jere Brophy. International Academy of Education & International Bureau of Education.

Timperley, H., Wilson, A., Barrar, H., & Fung, I. (2007). *Teacher professional learning and development: Best evidence synthesis iteration* [Iterative Best Evidence Synthesis]. New Zealand Ministry of Education. https://www.educationcounts.govt.nz/__data/assets/pdf_file/0017/16901/TPLandDBESentireWeb.pdf

Wei, R. C., Darling-Hammond, L., Andree, A., Richardson, N., & Orphanos, S. (2009). *Professional learning in the learning profession: A status report on teacher development in the United States and abroad*. National Staff Development Council.

Weinstein, Y. & Sumeracki, M. (with Caviglioli, O.). (2018). *Understanding how we learn: A visual guide*. Routledge.

Wiliam, D. (2014, July). Redesigning School – 8: Principled assessment design. SSAT (The Schools Network) Ltd. Retrieved 20 September 2020, from https://webcontent.ssatuk.co.uk/wp-content/uploads/2013/09/RS8-Principled-assessment-design-chapter-one.pdf

Wiliam, D. (2016). *Leadership for teacher learning: Creating a culture where all teachers improve so that all students succeed*. Learning Sciences International.

Wiliam, D. (2018). *Embedded formative assessment* (2nd ed.). Solution Tree Press.

Index

A SAGE Publishing Company

CORWIN HAS ONE MISSION: to enhance education through intentional professional learning.

We build long-term relationships with our authors, educators, clients, and associations who partner with us to develop and continuously improve the best evidence-based practices that establish and support lifelong learning.

Leadership That Makes an Impact

**MICHAEL FULLAN &
MARY JEAN GALLAGHER**

With the goal of transforming the culture of learning to develop greater equity, excellence, and student well-being, this book will help you liberate the system and maintain focus.

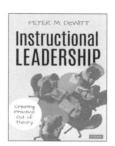

PETER M. DEWITT

This step-by-step how-to guide presents the six driving forces of instructional leadership within a multistage model for implementation, delivering lasting improvement through small collaborative changes.

BRYAN GOODWIN

If you've ever wondered anything, really—just out of curiosity—then you have what it takes to lead your school to restored curiosity and your students to well-being and success.

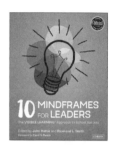

**JOHN HATTIE &
RAYMOND L. SMITH**

Based on the most current Visible Learning® research with contributions from education thought leaders around the world, this book includes practical ideas for leaders to implement high-impact strategies to strengthen entire school cultures and advocate for all students.

**DAVIS CAMPBELL &
MICHAEL FULLAN**

The model outlined in this book develops a systems approach to governing local schools collaboratively to become exemplars of highly effective decision-making, leadership, and action.

**MICHAEL FULLAN,
JOANNE QUINN, &
JOANNE MCEACHEN**

The comprehensive strategy of deep learning incorporates practical tools and processes to engage educational stakeholders in new partnerships, mobilize whole-system change, and transform learning for all students.

**JOANNE QUINN,
JOANNE MCEACHEN,
MICHAEL FULLAN,
MAG GARDNER, &
MAX DRUMMY**

Dive into deep learning with this hands-on guide to creating learning experiences that give purpose, unleash student potential, and transform not only learning, but life itself.

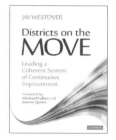

JAY WESTOVER

The transformative framework outlined in this book creates a districtwide approach for changing the culture of learning and creating a coherent system of continuous improvement.

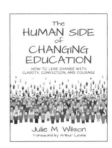

ANTHONY KIM, KEARA MASCARENAZ, & KAWAI LAI

This guide provides battle-tested practices to help leaders build better habits for team learning, meetings, and projects, to achieve a more responsive, innovative organization.

EVAN ROBB

Build the foundations of effective leadership despite daily distractions. Learn how to intentionally use ten-minute opportunities to consider and execute your vision.

AMY TEPPER & PATRICK FLYNN

Nineteen strategies help leaders, coaches, and teachers improve their ability to identify desired outcomes, recognize learning in action, collect relevant evidence, and develop effective feedback.

JULIE M. WILSON

Learn to make sense of challenging change journeys and accelerate implementation with this practical framework that includes human-centered tools, resources, and mini case studies.

GRANT LICHTMAN

Our rapidly evolving world is dramatically impacting how we view schools. *Thrive* shows educators how they can help their schools not only survive but thrive during rapid change.

ERIC SHENINGER

The future-forward framework in this book prepares leaders to harness the power of innovative ideas and digital strategies to create relevant, engaging, and intuitive school cultures.

CHRISTINE MASON, PAUL LIABENOW, & MELISSA PATSCHKE

Envision and enact transformative change with an iterative visioning process, thought-provoking vignettes, case studies from exemplary schools, key strategies and tools, and practical implementation ideas.

KIRSTEN RICHERT, JEFFREY IKLER, & MARGARET ZACCHEI

Shifting empowers educational change leaders to proactively and coherently navigate complex, unprecedented change in schools and establish a school culture in which changemakers can thrive.